T0275065

LILLIPUT
LAND

ADVANCE PRAISE FOR THE BOOK

'*Lilliput Land* says it like it is and is an excellent reality check on the Indian market opportunity and what it takes to win here. It offers fresh perspectives, new insights and sharp analysis that Rama Bijapurkar is known for, and is valuable reading for those new to India and those already here'—Anand Mahindra, Chairman, Mahindra Group

'It is the mastery of consumer insights, and the ability to read data and connect the dots into an Indian consumption story that makes *Lilliput Land* such a fascinating read! Rama's decades of analysis, practice, and teaching consumer research and market insights woven with nuggets of stories shine through, and make this book a must-read for anyone interested in the backbone of the Indian economy as well as young marketers'—Suresh Narayanan, Chairman and Managing Director, Nestlé India Limited

'In the dynamic landscape of the digital world, start-ups wield immense potential to revolutionize India's economy by addressing critical challenges through innovative solutions grounded in deep consumer insights—be it via new business models or leveraging the power of technology.

Rama's book is the ideal starting point to understand this. It brings forth India's consumption story and its drivers backed up by data-driven insights, and highlights the power of digital solutions that allow for solving real challenges at an affordable price, thus enabling businesses to unlock India's mass opportunity'—Falguni Nayyar, Founder and CEO, Nykaa

LILLIPUT LAND

How *Small* Is Driving India's Mega Consumption Story

RAMA BIJAPURKAR

PENGUIN
BUSINESS

An imprint of Penguin Random House

PENGUIN BUSINESS

USA | Canada | UK | Ireland | Australia
New Zealand | India | South Africa | China | Singapore

Penguin Business is part of the Penguin Random House group of companies
whose addresses can be found at global.penguinrandomhouse.com

Published by Penguin Random House India Pvt. Ltd
4th Floor, Capital Tower 1, MG Road,
Gurugram 122 002, Haryana, India

First published in Penguin Business by Penguin Random House India 2024

Copyright © Rama Bijapurkar 2024

All rights reserved

10 9 8 7 6 5 4 3 2

The views and opinions expressed in this book are the author's own and the facts
are as reported by her which have been verified to the extent possible, and the
publishers are not in any way liable for the same.

ISBN 9780143465492

Typeset in Bembo Std by Manipal Technologies Limited, Manipal
Printed at Replika Press Pvt. Ltd, India

This book is sold subject to the condition that it shall not, by way of trade
or otherwise, be lent, resold, hired out, or otherwise circulated without the
publisher's prior consent in any form of binding or cover other than that in
which it is published and without a similar condition including this condition
being imposed on the subsequent purchaser.

www.penguin.co.in

Why *Lilliput Land*?

The title of this book is borrowed from *Gulliver's Travels*, an eighteenth-century classic by Jonathan Swift describing Gulliver's adventures in the imaginary land of Lilliput. While many higher-order and nuanced interpretations of this novel exist, I have always loved the straightforward, literal story of a land of small-sized people together overpowering the giant Gulliver, who is many times bigger than any of them. It has always seemed to me a perfect, albeit simple, metaphor for India.

When the BRICS report from Goldman Sachs first came out in 2001, I was struck by the point it made that in the future, the world's largest economies may not be the world's richest economies. And that exactly describes India, which today has the clout of being the world's fifth-largest economy, on track to becoming the world's third-largest economy by 2030. Yet, today, it ranks well below 100 in the world in terms of per capita GDP, an indicator of how rich each Indian is. Even with the kinder metric of Purchasing Power Parity (PPP), India's rank improves only slightly.

As a corollary, India's mega consumption story, one of the largest and most exciting in the world, has Lilliput-like characteristics too. It is a story of lots and lots of small consumers earning and spending just a little bit individually that adds up to an enormous amount. They are served by millions of small suppliers, oozing innovation, agility and customer intimacy that is the envy of large companies. The whole ecosystem is powered by an unparalleled digital infrastructure that seamlessly supports billions of small transactions every day.

All this results in very challenging business economics made tougher by India's heterogeneity and geographical scatter, further compounded by the fact that 'modest income' and 'small' consumers do not mean 'un-evolved' or willing to settle for the suboptimal. Quite the contrary. Over the years, large companies have felt the pain of serving this Lilliput Consumer India—high on expectations, low on income, with mostly small ticket sizes. Except for a handful, many companies have retreated to serving only consumers at the top of the income pyramid, thus playing in a tiny fraction of the total opportunity. These consumers too have Lilliputian incomes compared to even the average income in developed markets. 'Lilliput Land' has given many an MNC 'Gulliver' a run for its money.

What's changed in recent times is the advent of digitally led, new-economy business models in other parts of the world. Businesses like Alibaba, Amazon, PayPal, DoorDash, Airbnb, Uber, Instagram and several others, particularly in services sectors like education, healthcare and logistics have provided clues of how to profitably play in the Indian market. They have inspired a flurry of vibrant Indian start-ups, the common thread being the digital business model capable of building profitable scale by bringing together the small—scaling up supply by aggregating small suppliers, scaling up demand by aggregating small consumers and scaling up the addressable market by enabling sharing of high-value products and services by lots of small users. This is the future of competition in Lilliput Land. Large platforms comprising myriads of small consumers and suppliers digitally yoked together, will drive the future of India's mega consumption story.

The title Lilliput Land: How Small Is Driving India's Mega Consumption Story *and this book are both dedicated to India's small consumers, small suppliers and small transaction digital warriors who have together built and will continue to build the world's most watched and least understood mega consumer markets. Let's stop waiting for the coming of age of India's consumer markets. That happened a while ago.*

Contents

1

God Is in the Detail

INDIA IS THE LAND of many truths—all true. It has lived for over four centuries.

Like the proverbial curate's egg, it is good in parts and like India's favourite comfort food, the khichdi, it is an amalgam of many disparate grains.

India's Long Walk to Recognition

India's stock in the eyes of the world has soared in recent times and will almost certainly continue to rise in the years to come. When it was born in 1947, India's survival itself was a question mark in the developed world, especially in Great Britain. Its economic transformation in 1991 from a socialist economy to one that embraced a free market was viewed with equal scepticism by global businesses in the developed world. India's coming of age as a remote services powerhouse for information technology at the turn of the millennium, amidst the Y2K scare that gripped the world, earned it new respect. However, until very recently, the status of being one of the key players and shapers of the world's economy and geopolitics has eluded India, especially in the eyes of the developed world. While China was rightfully seen to be in a league far beyond India on this count, it used to be par for the course for visiting global business teams exploring emerging markets to extol the virtues of Vietnam and ask when India would catch up—even though India's GDP was so many times higher.

Today, things have changed in terms of how the world perceives India. Even the historically unfriendly Western media have thawed their frosty disapproval and fully acknowledged, albeit grudgingly, India's recent achievements—be it the steady economic growth that has made it the fifth largest economy in the world, the new-found geopolitical adroitness demonstrated in its G20 presidency, the most impressive landing on the moon at a cost lower than the Hollywood blockbusters about space travel, or the visionary, vast and inclusive public digital payment infrastructure that is unparalleled in the world.

All this, coming as it does, at a time when China's economic miracle has hit a few speed bumps and its politics has become more worrisome, is making global businesses look at India with renewed interest and, hopefully, fresh eyes as an inevitable destination for increased investment.

This is very gratifying to many Indians who have struggled to market India to the world since 1991 when India embraced globalization and aggressively sought inbound investments for its domestic market and a share of overseas markets for 'made in India' goods and services.

Since those early days of India's economic rebirth, a lot of the world's distrust of 'made in India' goods and services has evaporated. In fact, in many areas, India is seen to offer the 'next practice' after the best practice that the world has known so far. However, what remains is the scepticism in the minds of businesses about India's domestic demand and their reluctance to place big bets on it or invest heavily in it. This, despite India being the world's most populous country with more than half of its population below the age of thirty and despite India being the fifth largest economy in the world with a demonstrated track record of sustained GDP growth; and even though, unlike China, more than half of India's GDP is accounted for by domestic consumption.

To the world of global business, especially from the developed world, typically the Western world, India's domestic demand has a bad reputation of being notoriously hard to tap and make money from. And perhaps with good reason too. This book explains why and what it takes to win in the Indian market.

Why India's Consumer Market Gets an (Undeserved) Bad Name

India's consumer market has often been dismissed by the world, and often enough, even by its own business elites, as 'has potential, shows promise, but not there yet'. To be fair, India's sales pitch for foreign investment in the first two decades after liberalization focused on the future potential of its consumer market and maintained that while it was still small, it was guaranteed to explode soon. But today, three decades after liberalization, even when the performance of India's consumer market has fulfilled the promises made about its potential on so many counts, the verdict and label of 'not there yet' have not gone away.

The 'not there yet' verdict is usually based on milestones and metrics created by global business consultants, who believe that there is a universal path of evolution—hence a singular pattern of development—that all markets in the world follow. India has defied this theory and evolved and developed in its own way; and because it did not match up to the global norms of what a developed market should be like, it did not get the benefit of the doubt or the investment depth it deserved. For example, conventional wisdom has it that there is a globally proven threshold of average per capita income that a country must have for its consumption/consumer markets to take off and on that count, India is seen to be not there yet.

However, several successful big and small businesses in India have stood this flawed idea on its head, and innovated products and business models to crash the cost of supply and offer consumer-delighting performance at consumer-affordable process, profitably. This has enabled consumption to 'take off' at far lower per capita income levels than ever experienced by the developed world. To take another example, India's retail environment has often been dismissed as not being evolved enough because of the millions of small so-called mom-and-pop shops spread around the country. Everywhere else in the world, small shops gave way to large-format modern physical retail very early in a market's development journey. India has performed poorly on this metric of market evolution. Its mom-and-pop retail shops continued to flourish, grow and serve consumer needs better—using cell phones, WhatsApp and digital payments. Distribution supply chains went digital decades ago, making even the smallest, remotest shop's sales and inventory visible. India has leapfrogged and mostly bypassed the era of large-format physical modern retail. The same small shops are now networked and even more digitally empowered, and are being serviced by a new breed of digitally smart wholesale distributors offering a range of services that are value-added and increase return on investment (ROI) for all the participants in the chain. All this is happening alongside vibrant e-commerce and the hybrid 'phygital' business model (e-commerce platforms supplemented by networks of small stores) is emerging as the way to win in the Indian market of the future.

'Not there yet' was also the verdict given on the Indian consumers' sophistication and ability to appreciate the value of brands, based on the metric of (poor) sales of global brands which are famous elsewhere. The fact is that India has had an increasing number of successful home-grown brands in both B2B and B2C markets that consumers perceive as adding more value to them. The Indian market has been seen as yet to develop because it is mostly below the developed market norm, or even the norm of other emerging markets, when it comes to the per capita consumption of a range of popular consumer goods, like breakfast cereal or Tetra Pak milk. The fact is that Indians have less expensive options for both that they perceive as being better. Yet India laps up global brands of cell phones. Another popular metric of consumer evolution is the extent of the Westernization of a culture. India has been a laggard on this metric because it has practised, over millennia, how to absorb external influences and evolve in its own unique way. Market analysts have often commented on the slow transition of Indian women from traditional Indian wear to Western wear, using that as a metric of consumer modernity. What they miss is the fact that a near-universal modern Indo-Western look has emerged across India comprising knee-length or longer tunics worn on top of leggings or various kinds of Indo-Western trousers. Indian women have already embraced, en masse, the benefits of convenience and mobility of Western wear while retaining the social and physical comfort of traditional Indian wear.

Indian and global business analysts have constantly benchmarked and compared the Indian market to other markets in the developed Western world or to Mexico, Vietnam or China and pronounced it to be 'not there yet'. In the meanwhile, India has evolved in its own leapfrogging, indigenous way and marched to the beat of its own drum. It is amply proven now that the Indian market will never become like 'someplace else, somewhere else'. It is also very clear now that the ugly duckling Indian consumer market, contrary to expectations, will not transform into the familiar beautiful swan of Western developed markets; instead, it has transformed into its own version of a big, valuable ugly duckling. It needs to be understood on its own terms and not in comparison to any other place or based on any stock theory of market evolution. As C.K. Prahalad wrote in the foreword to the first book of this series, *We Are Like That Only: Understanding the Logic of Consumer India*, 'Consumer India has its own logic, listen to the logic of Consumer India, from within.'

India's Orbit Change and the New Thinking on Global Business Strategy

Triggered by several steady changes that have compounded over time, India has now gained a size and clout in the world that can't be ignored. Three big things have happened. Today, India's ranking in the world both in terms of population (rank 1) and size of the economy (rank in nominal gross domestic product, or GDP) is very high, and it is consistently among the fastest growing countries in the world. The symbiotic effect of population and GDP is now kicking in, giving India an unprecedented heft in the world, hard to deny or dismiss. The third big thing is that India now has an enormous digital quotient, and the cell phone, the internet and a variety of digital technologies now form its central nervous system. Just as an illustrative data point, India has the largest number of internet users in the world and the largest number of digital payment transactions in the world. This new 'digital first' way of working has had many spin-off effects, ranging from distinctly reduced corruption in all spheres to enabling easy access to government services, building a modern welfare state with direct benefit transfers and targeted subsidies, making people more productive by making up for bad physical infrastructure and much more that will be discussed later.

But the most exciting benefit of India's high digital quotient, from a consumer market's point of view, is that after years of struggle, companies will now find it easier to profitably serve India's mass market. The hitherto high cost of serving a massive, modest income, geographically scattered, demanding consumer base has dramatically dropped, enabling companies to offer consumer-perceived delight at consumer-affordable prices and still be profitable. The argument that Indian household income levels are 'not there yet' at the so-called 'consumption take-off point' now doesn't hold much water, as digital-first start-ups in India are demonstrating every day.

The big changes inside India are fortuitously coinciding with changes in the external geopolitical environment, making space for India to use its new strength to force its way into places and money pools that it has previously had to struggle to be a serious contender for. Here too, from a business point of view, the most interesting new development is the change in discourse around the world on how to build and manage global businesses. The idea of a singular global strategy to be rolled out uniformly across the world is being replaced by the idea of more granular globalization, multiple country-level strategies, and the reluctant acceptance that different markets need different strategies and one size doesn't fit all. Therefore, deviant India, the child that did not fit naturally anywhere, is now being increasingly liberated by global companies and treated as a stand-alone region and not a part of ASEAN (Association of South East Asian Nations) or MENA (Middle East/North Africa) or any other geographic collective. It now does not necessarily have to make do with business strategies that were not tailor-made to unlock its enormous overt and latent potential.

This orbit change has huge implications for businesses, whether they are well entrenched in India, are cruising along in low gear or have a token presence in India while they wait for the ugly duckling to transform. This is also true of businesses who are watching and evaluating the India opportunity from the outside. Everyone has to pause and reassess their dominant logic about India—their business ambitions, their investment plans, strategic postures and business and market strategies—

if they are to seize the new and sustained opportunities that this orbit change brings. It is the coming of age of one of the biggest, fastest-growing consumption markets of the world with a very small number of players, an underserved market with an enormous consumer base raring to consume, albeit on its own terms. And it has taken three decades to get here, from 1991, when the nation opened up its economy and embraced market capitalism.

So Where's the Catch in Betting Big on India's Consumer Market?

The metanarrative about India is, fortunately, now not in question. A large economy, India is the fifth largest economy in the world in nominal terms or the third largest if you believe in Purchasing Power Parity or PPP. (One acerbic Fortune 100 CEO visiting India said that he could only consolidate 'real money' into his global profit and loss statement so please, no PPP!) The Indian economy has proved that it can weather storms and grow steadily, as indeed it has, even in the aftermath of the 2008 global financial crisis and the COVID-19 years. In a decade or so, India is likely to add another India to itself in terms of GDP. It harbours a large chunk of the earth's future adult population and a large chunk of future consumption growth, given that over half of its GDP comes from household consumption.

Whenever I have to make a presentation to visiting boards of global companies or at an investor conference selling India, I wish I could stop with just the one slide that shows the wonderful macros. But in truth, India's story is a bit more complicated. There have always been two broad narratives about India—the glass half empty and the glass half full, the beautiful, valuable, rare Fabergé egg and the curate's egg, only good in parts. It doesn't help that India is a land of contrasts, a nation that has lived in over four centuries at the same time. To many in India who are charged with selling India as an investment destination overseas, this half-empty–half-full description seems passé. They make the point (factually spot on) that never before in human history has such a vast swathe of humans seen so much positive change in such a short time. They provide statistics, all true, of how India has moved to the forefront of the world on many counts (digital transactions, unicorns, amount of red tape cut, foreign direct investment, GDP growth rate post-COVID etc.), and how this is the environment in which the world's most exciting consumer demand story sits. Despite such a compelling case for India to be the foremost global investment destination of choice, not everyone is a believer, and a fair share of sceptics abound. Even Indian–owned India Inc. has not voted commensurately with its pocketbook in terms of investing in this enormous consumer demand, barring a handful of companies. Every time there is a cyclical slowdown in the economy and consumption, they say that they are not confident about investing in India's consumer demand and that the government must stimulate demand. I often ask them why they prefer investing in overseas markets and why they are not confident about the long-term future of their domestic market which harbours the world's largest, youngest population with steadily increasing incomes and very high aspirations for a better life, in the pursuit of which consumption is centre stage.

Why aren't facts being taken at face value? What's not to believe? It is the incredible diversity of India and how the large macro numbers are distributed that results in contrasting narratives that on-ground experiences bring, as the media, especially the Western media, are quick to point out. While the India fact pitch talks of moving ahead of France and the United Kingdom and soon Germany in size of GDP, a walk down many parts of India brings to mind the line from *Wizard of Oz:* 'Toto, I've a feeling we're not in Kansas anymore!' While the fact pitch talks about an enormous consumer spending of around $2 trillion per year, the reality on the ground is that a large part of it comes from consumers who have low incomes but high thresholds of acceptability on product or service features and performance, and are consequently hard-to-serve. Therefore, most businesses that have been in India for a while are still much smaller than they should be in a country with such a large GDP and so much consumer buoyancy. Every time a very talented CEO of a large consumer goods company retires at age sixty, I can't help thinking that were it anywhere else in the world, she would have the problem of plenty of board chairmanships of consumer companies to choose from; except that there aren't that many consumer companies of size and scale in India on offer.

The Fallacy of Searching for the 'Correct' Singular Narrative

Here's the irony. While everyone who even has a smattering of familiarity with India is aware that India is a land of contrasts and incredible diversity—and that, therefore, the land that can only be described with multiple narratives—business people seem to want to hear the definitive, singular 'correct' narrative about India, to the exclusion of all other narratives. This especially applies to the territory of this book: the opportunity offered by the Indian market.

Both Indian companies and foreign investors need to go beyond and behind the screaming headlines of competitive chest thumping ('India beats XYZ country to become the nth largest economy in the world') or of reasoned alliterative sales pitches that position India as the 'it' destination for foreign investment (demography, democracy and demand) or the grudging often vicious 'yes buts' of the foreign media (the *Economist* in 2022 wrote about the vast national market, the brash new consumer class and the desperately poor internal migrants),[1] the endless cautions about how India is likely to be 'stuck in the middle-income trap', the disbelieving left economists and political factions who say the data is all fudged (reported GDP 7.19 per cent but feels like 5 per cent) or the dire warning of those who point out that society at war within creates a bad climate for business.

Rather than thinking in terms of a singular 'good news or bad news', 'ready for me, not ready for me' narrative, businesses keen on India need to embrace and process all the multiple narratives, gain insight and think in terms of the various levels of gain and pain embedded in the Indian market opportunity. Instead of choosing a singular truth about the 'Indian consumer' and finding that a strategy based on that truth has failed when rolled out across a diverse consumer base, it is better for businesses to think in terms of 'Consumer India', a nomenclature that acknowledges the enormous diversity of the consumer base with starkly different segments. The size of the prize (gain) is considerable and getting steadily bigger each year, but it requires a 'made for India' business strategy and execution, and multiple business models given the increasing heterogeneity of consumer India. Therein lies the pain.

Decoding the Multiple Narratives: God Is Found in the Detail

As with most things about India, God is found in the detail, and thinking in a segmented way is key to a robust understanding of anything to do with India, especially its consumer market and its consumer base that are the underpinning of India's consumption story.

Example 1: India's age demographics are great, but education and education for employability are really poor. 'Demographic dividend', enthuses one narrative; 'demographic disaster', intones another. The detail is that about half of young India is able to seize opportunities of entrepreneurship, go global to many countries East and West, and benefit from new sectors and new job opportunities, like becoming influencers, video jockeys, vets and coders. They are also able to access information, guidance and connections from well-off, well-educated India and climb the ladder to a better life. The other half typically come from poor rural homes and have very poorly educated parents. They have low risk-taking ability, a mediocre education and no knowledge about upskilling opportunities. This is what was originally labelled as India 1, India 2 and India 3 by retailer Kishore Biyani. India 1 is the India that has 'arrived'—it is well educated, has a profession or a business that makes them good money, is a favourite with the formal financial system for credit and has benefited the most from market capitalism. India 2 is the India that is connected to them or has made connections to them and benefited in various ways, while India 3 is the India that is left on its own, slowly trying to climb out of the well it is in without having any ropes of support thrown to them.

Example 2: Take another example, that of urbanization. Yes, urbanization is on the increase, as census data shows, but the same data also shows that 25 per cent of urban India lives in what are officially rated as slums. Data also shows that most of the urbanization has been from what the census calls 'census towns'—small towns that do not fit the official definition of 'rural' because three-fourths of the male workforce is not engaged in agriculture nor do they fit the definition of 'urban' because they do not have their own municipal body. Hence urbanization in India is more an artefact of how we define urban and rural in India, and is actually a phenomenon of de-agriculturization of rural India. This is different from the usual images one has from around the world of urbanization—people from villages moving to big cities to live better and earn better. In business plan meetings in India, an often-heard and used phrase that describes this twilight zone of urbanization is 'rurban' or 'semi-urban' or 'peri-urban'.[2] So, in effect, India's urbanization brings a different suite of consumer needs and desires. Peri-urban has been the sweet spot (easier growth avenues) for most urban-centric businesses to start going rural and vice versa.

True urbanization, as in rural people moving to big cities, also does happen and is creating higher incomes through various new avenues of work, though many would hesitate to describe these as 'value-added' jobs. They are better-quality and higher-paid informal jobs that do not exist in rural areas or very small towns, such as housekeeper-level maids, English-speaking and well-dressed nannies, dog walkers, party cooks who come and cook in your house on call, etc. If rural areas have disguised unemployment and hence low labour productivity, social infrastructure in urban India is improving too slowly to seriously improve labour productivity for the majority of rural migrants, who live in homes with poor access to basic amenities and space and poor transport.

To restate the obvious, contrasting evidence to prove diametrically opposite assertions is abundant, and deeper insight provides a better understanding of market segments and truly relevant needs as well as existing supply-side capabilities.

Example 3: Gurgaon or Gurugram, where a large chunk of corporate India is housed, is an interesting metaphor for India. The city was built mostly between 1996 and 2002 when private developers acquired 3000 acres of land on which they built stunning high-rise buildings and malls of the kind most Indians had not seen before. Bombay (now Mumbai) was the place everyone came to see high-rise buildings in the 1960s and 1970s, but after Gurgaon came up, it left even us Bombayites goggle-eyed and gawking—it looked like a foreign country. The so-called 'city' had no government amenities at all. All the utilities and public services, including even the fire brigade, were privately run. This was a poster child for what we say often in India—that the richer you are, the more you distance yourself from government services. Gurgaon got its first municipal corporation as late as 2008! In 2016, the *Guardian* ran a story titled 'Gurgaon: what life is like in the Indian city built by private companies'[3] and said that the wastelands have gone but the pigs have stayed. This was an exaggeration typical of foreign media reports but with a kernel of truth in it. The report said that the villagers who owned the land had been squeezed into ghettos near the highway and that the new Gurgaon private colonies had among the best homes in India and old Gurgaon among the worst. 'Entering a private colony,' the report said, 'is like crossing an international border'—like you are in America.

Around India, private housing of the rich and plush corporate office complexes are self-reliant in public goods, from security to electricity and everything else and interesting B2B and B2C islands of great value.

But the COVID-19 vaccination story showed us exactly the opposite. Despite the rich in India disconnecting themselves from government-provided services, the humongous COVID vaccination programme that India conducted was entirely state-run and tightly controlled digitally by the government, allowing no avenue for the rich to bypass the system and do their own thing or crowd out the poor. The rich went to government primary health centres, the poor to fancy private hospitals—wherever the app offered you a slot. I remember thinking at that time of the quote, 'A developed country is not a place where the poor have cars. It's where the rich take public transport.' So which is the real India? Both would be the right answer.

Example 4: This story from my WhatsApp group (all Indians belong to at least one WhatsApp group, the number often going up to double digits) illustrates the many conflicting truths, all true, that data can throw up, especially in the hands of argumentative Indians, and how data needs to be interrogated carefully.

An article titled 'Smart pickup in good jobs'[4] that appeared in *Business Standard,* a leading newspaper, based on data from a well-respected think tank was posted on the group. The article, published in November 2022, had data that showed that listed companies had added one million jobs that year, a number which might easily offset the recent lay-offs seen in the tech companies. Listed companies, the article explained, are the best employers and create high-quality jobs, so this data shows that there is a significant improvement in the quality of employment in India.

Several posts appeared in response saying that good news was here at last and the economy was breaking through to the next level, and this should boost consumption in a big way.

Then came a rejoinder that said:

India has 308 million families, less than 10% of whose chief wage earners are employed formally, and an even smaller percentage are employed by listed companies (of which there are only about 7500 in India). 33% of Indian households are dependent on casual labour and India's labour force is a whopping 540 million with growth coming from the villages. So one million jobs added is definitely a million jobs more than before, and good news, but it doesn't even remotely transform the quality of employment in India and give rise to a whole new genre of consumption.

Another post nuanced this interpretation by saying:

This is very good news for the top (richer) half of India which is indeed thriving and good news for India's GDP growth because they are big consumers. But these jobs added do not impact the poorer half of India which continues to struggle with poor quality or low or no employment and most of them were self-employed anyway.

Replied another, challenging this data:

Not true that the poorer half of India is doing badly, look at all the cell phone statistics and increased data usage in rural India. So, clearly, people are far better employed than the large proportion of casual labour or grade 4 (low-level white collar) jobs that employment statistics show.

And a rebuttal post to that which said:

> Half of India's rich live in rural India as do most of India's
> poor. So cell phone ownership increasing in villages doesn't
> always mean that the poor are buying. Besides, cell phones
> are available at all price points, calls mostly free and data very
> cheap, and owning one helps you earn. So it's not really a
> good metric of affluence.

That's just a glimpse of the argumentative Indian, of the many
data-backed truths, all true, needing to be made sense of when
assessing the market opportunity in India.

Prognosis: Curate's Egg, Khichdi and the Blind Men of Indostan

Three decades of liberalization and the flowering of the market
economy have resulted in India's heightened economic growth
(with different levels of benefit to different sections of Indians),
with a wholehearted embrace of the digital age. It has also brought
with it a wide swathe of social and polity changes (not all good or
all bad, for sure). Household and individual consumption, the 'C'
of the C+I+G (personal consumption expenditure + investment
+ government spending) that drive GDP, will continue to be
a very important determinant of India's economic growth and
stability. The chief economic advisor to the government of India,
when asked in an interview about what gives India strength in
this time of global turbulence, said, 'What gives us strength is the
fact that domestic consumption is the biggest driver of growth—
you are not exposed to or as dependent on global trade as, let's
say, for example, East Asian countries.'[5]

However, the new India continues and will continue to be like the proverbial curate's egg, good in parts. It will still be a khichdi of many Indias that have had different starting points and evolved in different directions at different speeds. Various other descriptions of India over the years still hold true: '. . . a geographical term . . . no more a united nation [single country] than the equator'[6] and '. . . not a real country. Instead, it is thirty-two separate nations that happen to be arrayed along a British rail line.'[7] India is a set of contradictory narratives and truths, all true. As Shashi Tharoor says eloquently, even with the motto on the government's crest 'Satyamev Jayate'—truth alone triumphs—the question remains, *whose* truth? So too for the Indian market and Consumer India.

To use another analogy to bludgeon the point home, India will, for a long time, be like the elephant in the story about the elephant and the blind men of Indostan who, depending on which part of the elephant they feel, declare it to be a wall, a rope, a tree trunk and so on. When I am asked to speak about the 'Indian Consumer', I rephrase it to 'Consumer India', to emphasize the diversity of the consumer base, and I prefer to be honest and reveal the whole elephant at one go—the rope, the trunk, the stolidity, and also the nimbleness and light-touch agility it has (ever seen an elephant reach for jackfruit high up in a jackfruit tree or heard its light tread on the grass?).

But the pushback is severe, especially from Indian business audiences and the media. They want to see the narrative of rich, urban, cosmopolitan, Westernizing India; the narrative of income growth, luxury goods sales, increase in upper-class working women with more autonomy in decision-making, and millennials and Gen Y who could be from 'anywhere in the world consumers who just happen to be in India'. Of course, there is enough evidence, all true, to support this narrative too, but it just doesn't add up to the entire GDP of India—it only applies to a fraction of it.

This book will unflinchingly and honestly paint the whole picture of Consumer India, the good and bad news, the counter-intuitive and the changing facets of it. It will slay beautiful hypotheses (and narratives) with ugly facts, to borrow a phrase from scientist Thomas Huxley. It will discuss what forces are shaping the future of this hydra-headed market and its consumer base. Since supply shapes consumer choices as well, it will discuss how this is playing with new economic models.

It will hopefully enable businesses to deliberate on what pain–gain ratio their company should go for and to choose 'my target India' based on fact and not one-sided narratives. It will also help businesses to think about what it takes to win consumers and best competition of all kinds, including small local competitors that are often dismissed as non-global, non-world-class but can be quite lethal.

This book provides the lenses with which to see a clear—less confusing, sharper, more specific—people-based map of the Indian market, and discusses the pain and gain of the Indian market opportunity so that businesses can make informed strategic choices. It provides far more insight than the spreadsheets of sales projections put out by global consultants that say 'by the year x, India will be the y largest market for z item'. This book provides an analytical lens with which to view all the anecdotal stories that appear in the media about the Indian market and consumers, and it explains the current and, likely, future supply landscape because supply shapes consumption as much as the other way around.

2

A Framework for Understanding Drivers and Shapers of India's Consumption

There are three drivers and shapers of the future of India's consumption story—the economic-demographic structure of Consumer India, how Consumer India behaves and what its mindset is, and what the supply side has to offer in terms of relevance and value addition to Consumer India's life. All three facets need to be read together to provide meaningful insight. The hero of the story is consumer behaviour, the villain is the structure of the consumer base and the supply side lags behind the consumer and has to catch up.

Consumer India
Structure Story

Consumer
Behaviour Story

Supply Side Story

The Case for a 'People-Level' Understanding of India's Consumption Story

IN INDIA, WE prefer to think of consumption in abstract terms, as a single, large, macroeconomic variable linked to GDP. We prefer not to think of it in human terms as the outcome of a large body of disparate people making individual choices about spending. Economy watchers think of consumption as an aggregate macroeconomic variable that drives GDP growth and is derived from revenues of companies, while business people or stock market analysts have the mental model that consumption is a macroeconomic tide that ebbs and flows, depending on GDP growth, and is responsible for lifting the revenue boats of businesses or dragging them down. Business plan presentations in India typically start with the GDP growth forecast as the basis for setting the annual target. At year-end, the blame for shortfalls in achievements against targets is often assigned to GDP growth being lower than what was forecast. It is not unusual for a company or an industry association to call on the government to give incentives to stimulate demand because sales are slow, their unspoken point being that demand creation is the job of economic policymakers, not of the marketing directors. What is missing in this 'consumption is a GDP-linked macroeconomic variable' view of the world is the idea that a business has many strategic and operational levers at its disposal to persuade consumers to buy and they should use them to swim against a slowing macro-consumption tide. This is especially true in an underserved, under-penetrated consumer market like India.

In the 'consumption is a macroeconomic variable' world view, there is no perceived need for any deep, or even perfunctory, understanding of the 308 million households that collectively make India's stellar consumption story happen. Forecasting the GDP growth is all that matters.

It is true that even without a people-level understanding of consumption and without the customer view in the C Suite, putting a reasonable (not dud) product into any part of the Indian market through any existing distribution channel will generate reasonable sales as surely as throwing a few stones at random in a public place in India is bound to hit a fairly large number of people. This explains why such a large, fragmented small-scale sector has always existed in many categories of goods and services, usually local or regional in scope. This is also presently the experience of several new so-called D2C (direct-to-consumer) brands distributed solely on large Indian e-commerce platforms. These brands have managed to muster sales revenues of even Rs 1 billion within two years of launch. The new darlings of private equity, many are yet to make a profit and the jury is still out on what maximum stable size they can get to this way, especially as more entrants play the same game and promotion costs become inevitable.

However, this is an almost inconsequential size of the prize in a country whose annual household consumption expenditure is larger than even the GDP of most countries in the world, and, more so, given how under-exploited and underserved Consumer India is (for more on why, see the chapter on supply, which explains supply evolution over time). The opportunity can be many quantum leaps greater and it can definitely be far greater than what is possible in many other developed or emerging markets around the world. India harbours enormous potential for new market creation by providing consumers or customers with new types of products and services to address a lot of unresolved pain and has offers of headroom to give customers better value than they are currently getting in several categories. What India offers today, in essence, is a large, fertile consumer base and a chance to get in early (like in an IPO or initial public offering) and build powerful business engines that can deliver long-term growth on autopilot as the economy grows.

Doing all this—i.e., designing businesses and developing strategies capable of capturing visible market opportunity and unlocking the enormous latent potential of the market— is possible only by going beyond the macro numbers and understanding the **structure** and the **behaviour** of Consumer India, comprising the 308 million households mentioned earlier. This includes knowing at a very granular level who they are, where and how they live, how they earn, how much they earn, what spending and saving choices they make, why and how they think and behave on several dimensions of consumption, the way they process value and so on. There is a third dimension that also needs to be understood alongside Consumer India's structure and behaviour, and that is supply, because suppliers also shape consumer behaviour and choices through their actions and inactions.

A Three-Part Framework for Understanding India's Present and Future Consumption Story

A good framework that I strongly recommend for understanding India's consumption story—where it is and where it is going or can go—is built around three areas: the **structure** of the consumer base, the **behaviour** of consumers and the structure of **supply** and the conduct of suppliers in their approach to serving Consumer India. This works well for understanding India's consumption at a country level as well as at the industry level or for company strategy development.

The Future of India's Consumption

Consumer India Structure story   ★ ★ 🐘

Consumer behaviour story   ★ ★ ★ ★

Supply side story   ? ?

India's future consumption story is set amidst a consumer base which has a socio-economic, geographic and demographic structure that is difficult to profitably serve, and which is unlikely to change in a hurry, a remarkable consumer behaviour across the board of consumption-seeking and aspiring, and a 'work in progress' supply side that lags behind the consumer in many ways.

While the rest of the book will provide a deep dive into each part of this framework, this chapter will offer a bird's eye view of what each part is about and of how all three parts, taken together, provide insight into India's consumption story.

I. The structure story of Consumer India

The structure story is all about having a solid socio-economic–geographic–demographic view of Consumer India in granular detail: How rich Indians are, how is income distributed, how is the income earned, where do consumers live, rich–poor, urban–rural proportions, who has access to infrastructure and who doesn't, education levels etc. This is something that we don't like to talk about a lot in India; in fact, it is something we prefer to ignore or view selectively because it forms the unglamorous foundations (a consumer base with modest income, modest education and poor living conditions) on which the glamorous macro consumption story rests (that we are among the largest and fastest growing market in the world, that fast-moving consumer goods or FMCG is to double in five years to $220 billion, that we are the world's largest two-wheeler market in 2022, with a size of $16 billion growing at about 10 per cent compounded annual growth rate etc.). Often, only a fraction of India's consumer base and the demand it accounts for, constitute the addressable market for many a company directly or indirectly serving Consumer India. This is because of their unwillingness to serve consumers at low per capita income levels and a wide geographic scatter, resulting in a long tail of demand.

The $5 trillion mark that the Indian GDP hopes to reach in the foreseeable future resides in various nooks and corners of the country. Half of India's household income is in rural India's 6,00,000 villages and only 18 per cent in the top nine metro cities with a population over 5 million.

The view of consumption through the structure lens is both depressing in terms of demographics—especially income and occupation—and confusing because of the incredible diversity. Understanding it properly requires honest, hard and quantitative information, not anecdotal behaviour-based assumptions. Rarely discussed in the context of consumption, despite their obvious influence on it, are facts such as that only around 20 per cent of Indian households have regular monthly salaries as their main source of income (as opposed to the majority, who are labourers, petty traders, small farmers and various kinds of small entrepreneurs who have no income predictability or security) and the even smaller proportion who have formal jobs (83 per cent of India's workforce is in the unorganized sector and 92 per cent are informal workers, i.e., those with no written contract and basic employment benefits like paid leave). The fact that over half of Indian Gen Y or Z or millennials are rural and have very modest incomes and old-fashioned dreams of a stable government job is also a blind spot kept blind in discussion on how Gen Y or Z are totally different from the generations before them and will adopt 'global' (Westernized) consumption practices.

II. The consumer behaviour story

The consumer behaviour story of Consumer India is about mindsets, perceptions and value logic that Indians have, and therefore, how they behave and how they choose. The structure story is a bit depressing but the behaviour story absolutely rocks, and has been celebrated in many media stories and books. Consumer India has a deep desire to consume everything, and a new god has been added to our large pantheon—the God of Consumption. Consumption has been morally purified (as has borrowing to consume) and is now seen as one of the legitimate goals of life—the combination of *artha and kama*! (two of the four life goals or pursuits of man in Hindu philosophy, artha being prosperity and kama being pleasure)!

The wrinkle in this upbeat story is that consumer behaviour in India is underpinned by limited income and an unlimited desire to consume. This influences consumer behaviour in ways that often stump marketers. For example, limited money and lots of desires lead to intense competition across categories wherein a vacation competes with a new large-screen home theatre or coaching class fees compete with eating out. It also leads to counter-intuitive value processing logic that makes Consumer India behave differently from consumers in many other markets. My favourite example of this, and one that I have shared in my first book *We Are Like That Only*, is about a lady who offered salon services at customers' homes. She was what marketing folks would categorize as being in between socio-economic class C and D, which is the lower-middle to lower-income category. She once told me that she subscribed to two pay channels for movies on her TV. I asked her why she chose to spend money on those when there were so many free channels already available for entertainment. She explained that she had two teenage boys at home, and if they were not incentivized to stay at home, they would go out, and being teenage boys, would spend money the moment they stepped out. So this was cheaper. Also, her mother-in-law would disappear to the neighbour's house or escape to her daughter's house to watch the newer movies that pay channels had. 'I need her to stay at home and manage the evening cooking and give the family dinner so that I am free to come for you working women, who are available only in the evenings but pay me more money for that.'

Another example of this is how many Indian consumers consider very small pack sizes to be more economical than larger ones, despite them being much more expensive per kilogram or litre. This is because smaller packs do not lock up money and since they have to be bought more often, consumers have more flexibility to delay replacement and hence, regulate consumption—B2B and B2C markets in India are abound with such interesting examples of counter-intuitive value processing by customers and consumers.

Data privacy is an issue everywhere, but in an affiliative and people-connected society like India's, most will willingly trade-off data privacy for efficiency, given how challenging the logistics of living are. I am what could be labelled as belonging to the segment of the 'educated upper class', and I do understand the need to guard my privacy and the dangers of not having it, but when I enter my apartment building with multiple doormen and liftmen, they tell me my cook has come, my yoga teacher came, waited and left, and note that my daughter hasn't come this weekend. Equally, I am sure that they are telling others about my movements and activities. However, they are the grease that smoothens my life, and I gamely smile and do nothing about it. On the other hand, I do not like e-commerce sticking bills with prices on the outside packaging of parcels for the same people to see and will change the store I buy from in order to not have my spending on public display.

The way Consumer India perceives value and demands it from products and services can make it less wonderful news for suppliers who can't match up to these demands. Its love for digital and its amazingly high digital quotient, despite poor education and low income, are a lesson reiterated yet again: poor doesn't mean backwards.

III. Supply as a shaper of consumption

Supply as a shaper of the future of consumption in India, is a factor which I have included for the first time in my analysis of India's consumption. This is because, for a variety of reasons that will be discussed in a later chapter, supply has neither kept pace with demonstrated demand nor has it created demand through relevant offerings that make consumers' lives better. The customer and consumer are way ahead of the supplier in their willingness to consume and in the multitude of unfulfilled needs that they have.[1] We just don't seem to have got our arms or heads around the enormity of our consumer demand. Even though a small fraction of India is flying, we are still battling long queues in most cities to even enter the airport, let alone go through security. Even in the small towns of India, finding parking space is hard.

In the late 1990s, when I worked with a leading global consulting firm, the firm's position was that 'people don't know what they don't know and so supply will create demand'. They heralded the impending explosion of organized modern trade and supermarkets and the diminished pull of traditional small retailers. The reality was of course quite different. Traditional small retail thrived because India's demand structure of high heterogeneity and small ticket sizes made the economics challenging for large-format modern retail and also because of the enormous customer-perceived value that the traditional retailer delivered compared to modern-format retail. Today, physical small retailers have grown and they exist alongside large and small e-commerce. The in-between stage of large-format modern (physical) retail has been pretty much bypassed.

When adding supply as the third factor besides the other two consumer-based factors that can shape consumption, I am not talking of a repeat of the 'build it and they will come' naiveté that we have seen and still see in many multinationals. More supply of the wrong kind will not boost consumption. The thirty years post-liberalization have been littered with corpses of multinational corporations (MNCs) that brought new supply to India that did not add value to the consumer and did nothing to boost consumption. Consumption happens when it is a solution to people's pain points or unresolved problems or offers better value (benefit minus cost) ways of doing the same things. Using this filter, the conclusion is that there has not been enough of the right kind of (relevant) supply to boost consumption. The e-commerce revolution that is hitting India is still focused around reducing the pain points of physical shopping but can do so much more to be consumption-boosting. For example, if someone acted on the pain point of painting our houses and offered a solution of speed and convenience, we would all paint our houses more often. Who hasn't stared at dirty walls and shuddered, despite having the money, grimacing at the tough choice between dirty walls and weeks of painter chaos? Going to the shop and buying new table mats is just so boring, and changing a small geyser for a bigger one for winter would be lovely. If there is a solution with two clicks and a guarantee or if there is an option where we don't need to sweat in the heat to get it, we would definitely choose that.

The cosmetics brand Nykaa says the ease of availability and buying as well as the excellent customer service they offer, have exploded the market for cosmetics in India. But it's a bit more than that: it's the ability to get one face-sculpting crayon in a pack of three that I otherwise need to buy, two of which are useless for me, or the bulk discounts available to a bunch of make-up services providers and influencers who can tell me what to buy and how to use it that creates demand, or that easy availability of a range of products and prices at one place ignites the latent demand in all women to hide their flaws and highlight their best features to look more attractive! IKEA is giving us so

many things that we couldn't have imagined earlier, and we are
buying because the relevant supply (right price–performance,
right value adding) is available. They have an amazing ultra-light
small laptop table that is so attractively priced, and easy to ship
and assemble that I bought three for my home—one for each
room for my family of corporate slaves who want to work in
the garden or verandah but don't want to lug tables and struggle
with propping up their laptops on books to get to the right
height and level of ergonomic comfort.

All of us, rich and poor, have now experienced chemicals
in our food—we have bought ripe-looking mangoes that don't
taste like anything or seen videos going viral of spinach grown
next to excreta on railway tracks. We are ready for genuinely
organic food or hydroponically grown greens, provided of
course that we can afford them or they are at a price that makes
us say '*paisa vasool*' (it's worth it).

India's consumption story will accelerate if there is more
consumption-boosting supply. Consumption-boosting supply is
about adding value to people's lives and making it worth their
while to consume. This is essentially the dharma of business
and the definition of marketing—adding value to people's lives
and extracting value from them. The greater the availability of
better benefits at an affordable cost, the greater the boost that
consumption gets. Biometric-enabled solar ATMs in rural areas,
adult diapers, telemedicine, and ready-to-eat pet food are just
some examples of relevant consumption-boosting supply that
we have seen of late in India. Reduce airfares, and the travel
market explodes, as Indigo has shown us. Please note, 'value
add' is not the same as 'price up'. The judicious combination of
benefit increases and price/cost of usage increases (or decreases),
as consumers or customers perceive it, makes for a consumption

increase. Chinese supply took Indian consumption by storm, offering never-before benefits at never-before prices. Think of the number of things Consumer India guzzled—nylon saris, children's shoes, battery-operated diyas for Diwali, noise-making shoes for walking in snake-infested village fields and so much more. As anthropologist Arjun Appadurai observed, the more you see by way of information, the more you are able to imagine a better life, with material objects playing a role in it.

With the invention of the shorter Western style 'kurti' or the tunic-shirt that covers the hips and ends mid-thigh or above the knee, as compared to the longer traditional kurta, young Indian women have been able to enjoy wearing jeans, or 'jean pant' as they call it, despite the conservative social milieu they come from that frowns on Western wear. When this trend was nascent, I used to joke with my client who had a large denim production facility that he should focus on stoking the kurti trend and keep it alive and vibrant (through longer t-shirts, for example) so that his denim investment would remain safe.

If GoColors, the apparel brand that makes stretch bottoms of every colour and kind hadn't appeared on the scene with its profusion of little neighbourhood stores, the way young women of all social classes now dress wouldn't have been so transformed. Their denim pull-up elasticated 'jeggings' have introduced even more Indian women to jeans of some sort. Ready-to-eat chapatis and rotis are yet to appear in any serious, robust way; when they do appear with wide availability at the right price-performance, a large part of the one trillion chapatis that Indians eat in a year will be eaten that way, and the size of processed or packaged food consumption in India will explode. The problem has not been with consumer resistance—south Indians don't know how to make chapatis, though they would like to eat them once in a while instead of their staple, rice, and most women in chapati-eating areas see making chapatis as negative labour (consumers often tell me how making chapatis, standing at a hot stove, is positive labour if you are making it for your children but negative labour if you are making it for your husband or mother-in-law). The consumer is willing, but where is the appropriate supply?

Even more fundamentally, the extent and nature of Consumer India's consumption depends, in equal measure, on both the income levels of Consumer India and the prices of consumer-acceptable supply. The desire to consume is so deeply embedded that it is not an issue any more. Consumption growth can happen in two ways: first, if prices of consumer-acceptable supply drop due to supplier actions (choosing to give up margin for increased volume or innovating to bring down price or more efficient supply chains etc.), thus enabling more consumers to buy, or second, if consumer incomes go up and they can afford to buy more things, or things that they previously could not afford to buy. A combination of the two will obviously be the best accelerator for India's consumption and unleash the consumption promise of the world's most populous market, where over half of the population is below the age of thirty, but whose GDP per capita rank in the world is 169. Chart 1 below visually shows the effects of the combination. In the late 1990s, this is exactly what happened. Incomes grew faster than ever before as the economy grew, post liberalization.

The celebrated telecom revolution in India, where even those with very modest incomes have smart cell phones and use data on them for streaming entertainment, has occurred thanks to the availability of cheap devices (a price of Rs 6000–8000 will get you a reasonable quality smartphone that gets the job done)

Chart 1: Combined effect of income and price

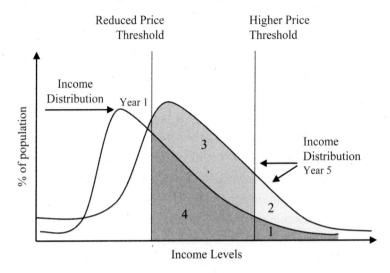

	Year 1 Income distribution	Addressable Market Year 5 Income distribution
Higher Price Threshold	1	1+2
Lower Price Threshold	4+1	1+2+4+3

and India has amongst the lowest telecom rates in the world. Depending on the plan you have, talk time and text messages are virtually free, and 1 GB of data costs Rs 5.00 ($0.07), as compared to the USA, where the cost of 1 GB is between $3–5 and the global average is of around $8.

Using this frame, it's easy to see that had Tata Nano been a more acceptable product to the customer, the drop in the price threshold for buying a car and the rise in consumer incomes of the target group over time would have moved the market very quickly from two-wheelers to cars. Or, more likely, more two-wheeler owners would have been buying cars in addition to their two-wheelers and more higher-income parents would have bought it for their children as a safer option than a two-wheeler.

Between 1995 and 2005, this is exactly what happened in India. Per capita income (net national income/NNI) grew 1.6 times. At the same time, the prices of most things came down on account of increased competition and also the reduction in taxes on consumption (consumer goods were taxed heavily pre-1991, as many items were considered to be 'luxuries' consumed by the rich). Competition increased because of the freeing up of the 'License Raj' market, allowing new entrants from the private sector to come in, and that caused both an improvement in quality and a decrease in prices, and an explosion in consumption.

Taken together, these three areas of consumer structure, behaviour and supply also provide a sound explanation for the confusing demand patterns

Often sales data throws up consumer behaviour that suggests a capricious, whimsical Consumer India. Sometimes 'uptrading' happens, and higher price-performance products grow faster, and sometimes the reverse happens and 'downtrading' occurs to lower price-performance points. Many theories abound, but a deep analysis of which part of Consumer India is doing what and why is the only way to know what is actually going on. For many years, first-time buyers of cars bought a particular category of cars, and then the 'same segment' of first-time buyers started buying a higher category of cars. The reason is that multiple segments of first-time buyers have emerged over time in addition to the original segment of those whose families never owned cars before and are now upgrading from two-wheelers. New buyers now include a larger group than earlier of children of car-owning families buying their first car and there is a growing segment of enterprising young men in touristy small towns who discover that there is an opportunity to buy a good SUV for the increasing numbers of well-heeled tourists who want more comfortable travel and easily manages a bank loan for it.

Sudden drops in auto sector sales in the past have not been due to households buffeted by economic headwinds, as popularly assumed, but because of banks hitting their limit of bad loans (non-performing assets or NPAs) and stopping their lending to aspiring Uber and Ola drivers or aspiring private transport operators. Auto sector sales always bounce back, even as the companies and television anchors are wringing their hands saying that slowing sales are on account of slowing GDP growth. This is because only the richest 10 per cent of India buys cars, and they have enough surplus income and car loans on tap at low rates, so their behaviour is driven more by sentiment ('let's postpone the purchase unless there is a good enough reason to buy now') than by income earned.

Rural India, which is poorer than urban India, laps up SUVs and large-screen televisions. This is because half of India's richest 20 per cent of families live in rural India, while 70–80 per cent of India's poor live in rural India. I remember once doing a survey on two-wheelers and finding that the upper-income buyers were buying the cheaper, more basic category of motorcycles, while those with much lower incomes were buying the more expensive models at higher price-performance points. Of course, everybody's first reaction was 'Check the data, the fieldwork has gone awry'. But investigating this through the structure and behaviour lens, we found that more than half of car owners in India also own a motorcycle. So when you want to show off and signal superior status when taking the family to a wedding, for example, you use the car, and the motorcycle or scooter is used for going to the office or for everyday running around—a cheaper, more utilitarian two-wheeler brand will do. However, if the two-wheeler is your sole vehicle, and your comfort and your status signals also need to come from that, then buying the more expensive bike is necessary.

3

Making Sense of the Structure Story

Consumer India's structural characteristics are a mix of good and bad.

Being the most populous nation on earth and hugely diverse, many versions of India coexist.

Overwhelmingly young, but nowhere near as rich as we imagine the world's fifth-largest economy to be—low on formal education, high on digital ability, mostly informally employed and low-skilled.

Even a small fragment of India is larger than most countries of the world. Companies need to understand Consumer India's structure story to decide which Indias to cobble together as 'my target India' and align their ambitions and strategy accordingly. There are plenty of choices available.

Psychological Paths of Least Resistance
Morgan Housel, 9 March 2023
(collabfund.com)

5. The desire to supplant statistics for stories

"People would rather believe than know", said biologist E.O Wilson.

I think . . . people desire stories more than statistics . . .

Part of that is good . . . It's because real-life stories are so effective at showing us what certain parts of a statistic mean.

Part of it can be dangerous, when broad statistics are ignored over powerful anecdotes.

When confronted with a pile of dull facts and a pile of compelling anecdotes, the anecdotes are always the path of least resistance for your brain to cling to.

This chapter has demographic data and data on income and income distribution by income segments, geography, occupation and education, drawn from a variety of sources

Beautiful Hypotheses and Ugly Facts

Income and occupation are two of the key elements of any consumption story—how much money consumers have and how they make that money (therefore how stable, resilient and growth-oriented is that money). And to the extent that occupation determines social status and lifestyle in India more than it does elsewhere in the world, it also determines the nature of consumption (is a laptop necessary, are curtains or rice cookers important and so on).

In most discussions on Consumer India, income is usually the elephant in the room. Nobody really likes to discuss it, possibly because the real numbers are so much lower than what we would like them to be, given our self-image is based on India's high GDP rank in the world. This often reminds me of a talk show I once saw, where someone was asked, 'How old are you?' and he replied, 'In years or in ¥ (Yen)?' Puzzled, the TV interviewer said, 'How can you measure age in ¥ (Yen)?' The man replied, 'I am fifty-four in years, but I yen to be twenty-two.' (Note for the millennial and Gen X, Y and Z readers! Yen is an old English word for a strong feeling of wanting or wishing for something.)

When told that even the richest 10 per cent of Indian households earned just Rs 21.6 lakh per annum in 2021 (details of how this number is derived follow later in this chapter), most readers will tend to be incredulous and unhappy. That doesn't sound right and doesn't sound good at all, more so when converted to US dollars. Intuitively, this figure is at odds with the large sales number of premium products that we see. However, 10 per cent of India adds up to a population that is the size of Mexico. Therefore, when BMW says India is the third largest country for its cars, it does not mean India is the third richest country in the world; rather, it reflects that a tiny share of India's large population is greater than a sizeable share of the small population in its other markets. iPhone, in the first half of 2023, is reported to have a (small) market share of 5.1 per cent of India's smartphone market but this translates to about 4 per cent of iPhone's global market.

Then there is the incessant talk everywhere extolling the rapid rise of India's middle class. Domestic and international media, publications of reputed global consulting firms and think tanks and especially India's investment pitches for foreign investment are all quoting numbers based on hearsay or vague and subjective judgements of some income or consumption levels that qualify a household to be middle-class or that fits a certain mental model of active, vibrant consumption of a certain premium-ness that we feel our middle class ought to have. Not only are there no uniform definitions in terms of income and consumption levels, but there are also no qualifying characteristics that the sociological definition of middle class usually implies, like the stability of income, surpluses to weather downturns, occupations and skills that provide resilience to bounce back from bad times. How rich is India's 'middle class', and how does this compare with the incomes of the middle class in other countries—a data point that global businesses have to consider?

Theories also abound on rural consumption growth, urbanization and what it means for consumption, and the rising incomes of tier 2 towns and several other geography-related stories. These are usually based on sales data and often have no underlying consumer-based explanation. What is the reality based on hard data? Spoiler: rural India is core to India's consumption story, urbanization statistics don't mean what you think they do and income is evenly distributed (scattered?) all over the country.

It is now time, as biologist Thomas Huxley said, to slay beautiful hypotheses with ugly facts. The rest of this chapter provides a detailed (some would say gory) data-based analysis of the structure of Consumer India with emphasis on income and occupation, and what insights this leads to about India's consumption story and what it takes to win in India's mega consumer market

Making Sense of the Tower of Babel on Household Income Data

Despite the critical need to understand household income in order to understand household consumption, there is no ready, 'official' source of income distribution data in India that everybody uses.

As with a lot of things in India, so too with income data, it is the Tower of Babel out there. There are many versions of household income data and many definitions of income classes that you will see in business presentations, media articles and investor pitches. The data varies depending on who is putting it out, which part of the income pyramid they are interested in and how they got their numbers (many, including glitzy global consulting company reports, don't say). Official income statistics are hard to come by in India because government data is around household expenditure and not income. Income tax data is not very helpful because only 8.1 million people pay income tax in India today. Even assuming one person per household (likely to be more) is earning, that leaves a data blank for 300 million households.

Why getting income data in India is such a challenge and data sources used in this chapter

Given the heterogeneity of Indian households on so many dimensions, surveys which are representative of all of Consumer India and also provide valid readings at disaggregated levels require large sample sizes and geographic spreads. This makes them expensive, elaborate, time-consuming and rare. On top of that, income measurement is tricky because only a minority of households have a steady monthly income, and even what constitutes income in a country with so many occupations and so much informal employment needs to be thought through and is difficult to survey using simple measures.

With these challenges, there are very few organizations whose income data is reliable enough. One of them whose data I analyse a lot is called the ICE 360 dataset from the think tank PRICE and it is generated from Pan Indian surveys conducted in 2014, 2016 and 2021. Its survey design and methodology are harmonized with the pioneering income-expenditure surveys done by the National Council for Applied Economic Research (NCAER) between 1995 and 2004 so that the data from both sources is comparable. (Disclosure: I was a promoter and founder of PRICE, but retired from it in 2022.) In addition, the Market Research Society of India and the Media Research Users Council are two industry bodies that conduct the industry-accepted socio-economic classification of Indian households using surrogate variables for income (affluence), such as ownership of durables and the occupation of chief wage earners. The appendix at the end of this chapter provides a more detailed version of this topic, with a discussion on different sources, their sample size, the methodology used for eliciting income data and income estimation methodology.

In this chapter, I have used the most reliable data sources in my assessment and they include ICE 360 income data, the data on the socio-economic classification system from the Kantar World Panel, the Media Research User Council and the National Sample Surveys. I am not a fan, as I have said in my earlier books, of any income estimates that use the 'comparable country' analogous income modelling for reasons beyond Indian exceptionalism. This approach is fraught with a lot of assumptions and no clear explanation of the comparability construct, especially given how fast the world changes between two points in time. India may have the per capita income that China or some other country may have had a decade ago, but much has happened in India in the intervening decade, and income distributions may have evolved very differently. India also has distinctly different economic and political growth drivers by state. There is no one national policy driven down and, therefore, many moving parts. Had Sonia Gandhi been prime minister, we may have had a very different pattern of income distribution than we do now.

Linking survey income data to the all-India Personal Disposable Income (PDI), the only household income statistic put out by the government in national accounts

As was said earlier in this chapter, for many people who use survey-based income data or are too sceptical to use it, the actual household income numbers that survey data throws up are disappointing and hard to believe since their ideas of household income have been shaped by the macro GDP number or the growth rates of sales for large companies. I have addressed the disconnect they experience between the micro (low household income levels) and the macro (large GDP) and tried to reconcile it in the following way (apologies in advance, I am going to get a bit technical here): I have used income distribution data obtained from the survey (what percentage share of all-India household income does each income group have, starting from the richest 10 per cent of households to the poorest 10 per cent) and applied it to the official government number of personal disposable income (PDI), which is the total income of all households in India net of taxes to get household level income. This way there can be no debate on whether survey-based household income numbers are 'true'. They gross up to the all-India Personal Disposable Income number, hence are not too low to believe. A more detailed explanation of this is available in the appendix titled 'Detailed Section on Household Income Measurement' for those readers who wish to get deeper into the methodology.

What is the most sensible way in which to define income groups for India, i.e., the best way to group households based on their income?

Reports and presentations that quote income data use a wide variety of income categories or groupings, the basis or logic for which is rarely spelt out. These groupings are often allotted cute labels like 'seekers', 'strivers' and 'aspirers', which seem to be, as my soldier brother would say of us MBAs, '*sirf angrezi*' (just English), meaning long on language and short on depth. This is because these labels are not genuine attitude segments which are data-based and analytically derived. Such faux labels can be misleading, making marketers read the wrong meaning into the essence of what drives each group. Does the 'seeker' group desire more experiences and superior products? Is the 'striver' segment households who have not yet got the economic clout to aspire? All Indian households are aspirers, aspiring for the next rung of the ladder of better living, to give their children an education that will give them escape velocity to a better life. To be fair, other more rational labels like 'next billion' are also used in reports, though not very often. A recent income report arbitrarily defined narrow income bands of 'near rich', 'clear rich', 'sheer rich' and 'super rich', who collectively account for a mere 3.5 per cent of all households, hair-splitting that delivers very little incremental consumer insight!

Then, there are the totally amorphous and highly popular labels like 'middle class'. In every one of my books, I have a section trying to demystify what the middle class is and I have one at the end of this chapter as well.

The new flavour of the year is the label 'Middle India', which seems to be the income class in the middle but is not the middle class, the way it is described or used popularly. Another popular term is the catch-all label of 'consuming class' (doesn't everybody consume, might ask Jio and Hindustan Unilever, whose consuming class comprises almost everybody).

In the rest of the chapter, different schemes of constructing income groups or income categories will be discussed, along with the logic for each; for each scheme, the number of households and the average household income in each category will be presented.

The idea is not to confuse readers with a data overload but to empower them to pick the scheme that best suits the strategic logic of the business or the reason why they are looking at income data. My friends who work in social development policy are always quick to remind me that they study income distributions for reasons that are different from business. Global businesses are looking at income with a global comparison lens, while mass-market rural players want to understand income distributions differently from urban premium market players.

Table 1: Household income levels based on PDI and NNI and GDP for each global income class (2021–22, nominal)

World Bank defined Global Income Class	Size and average income of each income class						
	Based on PDI			Based on NNI	Based on GDP		
	% of HH	Million HH	Average HH income (Rs lakh/ year)	Average HH income (Rs lakh/ year)	% of HH	Million HH	Average HH (Rs lakh/ year)
Rich	10	31	22	24	10	31	27
Upper Middle	20	62	10	10	20	62	12
Middle	20	62	5	5	30	92	6
Lower	50	154	2	2	40	123	2

HH: Household | PDI: Personal Disposable Income | NNI: Net National Income | GDP: Gross Domestic Product

Table 2: Income, expenditure, surplus income share by each group (2021–22)

World Bank defined Global Income Class	% share of all Indian household			Million HH	Pooled GDP of group* $ trillion	GDP per capita of group $
	Income Share	Expenditure Share	Surplus income Share			
Rich	36	27	68	31	1.2	8874
Upper Middle	31	30	32	62	1.0	3816
Middle	17	19	8	62	0.6	2120
Lower	17	23	-8	154	0.6	840

* All India Nominal GDP taken as $ 3.38 trillion; *Component of all India GDP resident in each income group

Way to read the table: Row 1: The global rich have 36 per cent of India's household income, 27 per cent of India's household expenditure and 68 per cent of India's surplus income, which is income minus routine expenditure of a household (which does not take into account one-off expenditures such as medical emergencies or social obligations). This income group has 31 million households. In the next two columns, for purposes of easy comparability across countries, the component of all-India GDP residents in each income group has been computed by multiplying the income share of 36 per cent by India's GDP in $. The global rich households in India have a $1.09 trillion 'GDP share', and the last column gives the average per capita per year GDP of this household. The remaining rows apply to the rest of the income groups. Family size has been taken as 4.4.

Section I: Understanding Income Structure by Income Group

Method 1: Aligning with the World Bank's global definitions of rich-upper-middle-middle-low-income classes

The World Bank defines four global income classes: low, middle, upper middle and high. These are based on the income levels of different zones or country clusters with similar levels of economic development. Taking a cue from a recent analysis published by PEW Research,[1] I have applied World Bank definitions[2] of the four income classes or groups to the ICE 360 survey data to generate a household income distribution for India which aligns with global income classes used by the World Bank.

Table 1 gives the percentage of Indian households that fall into each global income class as defined by the World Bank, using PDI as the total income of Indian households. I have also taken the liberty of showing what this would be if we considered total Indian household income to be either net national income (NNI) or GDP. GDP is a favourite affluence indicator in business—because most mental models of relative affluence across countries are based on GDP (even though it inflates the household income numbers! GDP is about 1.25 times PDI and NNI is 1.1 times PDI).

10 per cent of Indian households fall into the global rich category, 20 per cent into the global upper middle income, 20–30 per cent into the global middle and 40–50 per cent into the global low–income category, depending on the measure of total household income used.

The absolute income levels and number of households in each income class thus defined are also shown in Table 1.

Table 2 further profiles each World Bank-defined global-income class in India and presents the share of India's household income, expenditure and surplus income that is resident in the group. The globally rich 10 per cent of Indian households, 31 million in number, for example, have about 36 per cent of the total income of Indian households, just a bit more than a quarter of Indian household routine expenditure and two-thirds of total surplus income.

The table with the commentary below is self-explanatory and benchmarks India's income segments against global income classes defined by the World Bank. To further facilitate mental models that benchmark India against other countries, the table also presents a rough and ready estimate of 'GDP' for each segment (treating it like a 'country'), assuming that the share of GDP in the segment is the same as the share of income. It also then computes the per capita GDP of the segment. Therefore, the poorer half of India—the global lower income—has a collective GDP of $510 billion (about the size of Thailand and bigger than Vietnam), but with a nominal per capita income of only $756 per year which puts it in the bottom 10 per cent of the world country rankings. The global rich segment in India is a 'country' with a GDP of about $1.09 trillion, and a per capita income of $8015, in nominal terms.

Of course, the picture looks a lot better in PPP terms, which is the basis on which the World Bank has defined these income classes, but it is for readers to decide which they prefer depending on the reason why they are looking at this data and their India strategy—for example, local manufacturing versus imports, domestic market versus exports, consolidation with global accounts, etc.

Method 2: Keeping It Absolute, Not Relative. Using Income Quintiles and Deciles (20 and 10 per cent Slabs of Households Grouped according to Their Income) to Understand India's Household Income Structure

As discussed earlier, instead of arbitrary income cut-offs with English language-rich arbitrary labels, a more meaningful way of looking at income structure in India is to simply categorize it by income quintiles, or 20 per cent slabs of household income, until we do more research on income thresholds of significant change in behaviour and genuine behaviour or attitude-based segmentation.

Why are quintiles a good way to understand income distribution?

Chart 1 and Table 3 provide the answer. Chart 1 shows the income of each quintile from 1995 to 2021, with comparable data points whenever available through comparable methodology surveys of NCAER and ICE 360. Table 3 shows the share of income, expenditure and surplus income (income minus routine expenditure, not including one-off or occasional special payments such as social ceremonies, surgeries and medical emergencies, capitation fee for college admission etc.) by quintile as of 2021.

The chart and table show the following:

⇒ The richest or top 20 per cent of income earners are a distinct group—they are consistently and discontinuously higher earners as compared to the rest of the households, as can be seen from the chart. As Table 3 shows, they also have a disproportionately large share of income, expenditure and surplus income. This gives them the ability to bounce back easily and sustain lifestyles over economic slowdowns when incomes are either lower or growing slower. They actually fit the mental model that most people have of India's middle class and are the mainstay of consumption during economic slowdowns.

⇒ The top 40 per cent of households have a comfortable surplus income, and the difference between the top 20 per cent and the next 20 per cent also emerges clearly when analysed this way.

⇒ The poorest 20 per cent are a distinct group too. They are dis-savers, a group with negative surplus income or very marginal surplus income even in times of good economic growth. They are the group that welfare schemes are targeted at. Mahatma Gandhi National Rural Employment Guarantee Act (MNREGA), the rural employment guarantee programme, designed to be a self-selecting sample of the lowest income and unskilled Indians, served 57 million households in 2019 pre-pandemic, which is about 20 per cent of Indian households (most of the households in this category are in rural India). They are now also beneficiaries of the direct benefit transfer scheme of the government as well as several state and central welfare programmes and the dignity and assurance offered by the modern digitally powered welfare state that has been built in the last decade.

Chart 1: Income trends by quintiles over time

Income growth story

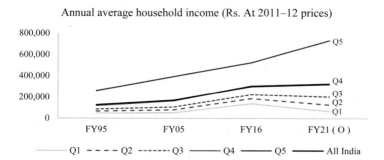

Annual average household income (Rs. At 2011–12 prices)

Q1: Poorest 20% | Q2: Second poorest 20% | Q3: Middle 20% | Q4: Next richest 20%
Q5: Richest 20% households

Table 3: Profile of each income quintile: Income, expenditure, surplus income share of all-India households resident in each quintile (2021)

% share of each group

Income Group defined by quintiles Q = Quintile	HH Million	% share of all Indian household			Surplus income to total income ratio for each group %[3]
		Income	Expenditure[1]	Surplus income[2]	
Q5 Richest 20%	61.6	54	44	92	35
Q4	61.6	22	24	14	13
Q3	61.6	13	16	0	0
Q2	61.6	8 ⎱ 24	11 ⎱ 32	(4) ⎱ (6)	-11
Q1 Poorest 20%	61.6	3	5	(2)	-13
Total All India	308	100%	100%	100%	21

1. Non-Routine expenditure one-off expenses (social, medical, educational etc. not taken into account | 2. Surplus income = Income minus routine expenditure. | 3. Ratio of absolute amount of surplus income to total income hosted

Therefore, it makes sense from an India-specific point of view to analyse Consumer India by income quintiles. There are logical categorizations that make more intuitive sense. It will also resonate with our own experiences for those of us who live here or who work on the ground in the Indian market.[3]

India's income structure as understood from a view based on income quintiles (refer to Table 3)

The richest 20 per cent of Indian households, given their share of income and expenditure and surplus income relative to the rest of the households, are the primary target group for most companies that are not comfortable with the low-margin high-volume pain of the mass market. As discussed briefly earlier in this section, it is this group of Quintile 5 (Q5) households that is actually India's 'middle class' in that it conforms to the mental model that most marketers have when they target India's middle class. Contrary to what many people assume, they are scattered everywhere, and half of them live in rural India.

The second quintile (Q4), comprising the second richest 20 per cent of Indian households, is also seen as attractive to marketers—even those who do not define themselves as mass marketers. They are the only other income group alongside Q5 with surplus income and accounting for a good chunk of household income and expenditure—20 per cent of the income and 24 per cent of the expenditure of all Indian households.

The middle two quintiles of Q3 and Q2 comprising the middle 40 per cent of households in the income hierarchy ranging from the 20th to the 60th percentile) actually form India's mass market with fairly similar characteristics of surplus income and similar income levels. It is this group that drives a lot of category growth for mass market fast-moving consumer goods (including occasional usage of premium segment products) and basic durables (including some higher priced utilities that help them to earn more like second-hand two-wheelers and basic smartphones).

The consumer base of the lower (by income) 60 per cent of all households in quintiles 3, 2 and 1 have no surplus income. This measurement has been taken post-COVID, but structurally, the pattern is the same as it was pre-COVID, though the situation is directionally much worse after COVID (a more detailed discussion of the COVID effect follows later in this chapter). The last column of Table 3 indicating the share of surplus income to total income shows that, for households in each income quintile, as of 2021, the middle quintile of Q3 just about breaks even while the bottom two quintiles are spending more than they are earning. This should be a metric to watch because surplus income will drive consumption significantly both in terms of having the money and in terms of the confidence to spend. Q3 even in non-COVID years has a marginal income surplus after expenditure but is easily set back with the slightest emergency. These 60 per cent are households at the base of the income pyramid and though they are therefore shaky and volatile as a consumer base, they still account for a quarter of India's income and a third of its expenditure. These groups will improve their income over time; to return to Chart 1, we see that in just fifteen years, the income level at which Q4 (the second richest 20 per cent households in India) was in 2005 is fairly close to the income level of Q2 (the second poorest 20 per cent) in 2021. As per our projections, had the pandemic not happened, Q1 (the poorest 20 per cent) in 2021 would have been at the same income level that Q4 (second richest 20 per cent) was at in 2005.

Within the top 20 per cent group that I sometimes call T20—to borrow a phrase from the popular IPL cricket matches—there is a super affluent category comprising the richest 10 per cent of Indian households who, even in the World Bank definition, qualify as 'global rich'. Their share of income expenditure and surplus income, disproportionate to their size, is self-evident in Table 4.

Table 5 shows the average household income level in each income group or income quintile (20 per cent slab of Indian households) in the second column. In the third column it shows the total pooled income i.e. the combined income of all households in that income group or quintile. This is the 'income worth' of the income group or quintile. The data in these two columns are calculated based on Personal Disposable Income or PDI. As discussed earlier in this chapter, for those who prefer to think in terms of GDP, taking the liberty of assuming that the GDP share of each quintile is the same as the PDI share, the GDP share of each income group and the per capita 'GDP worth' has also been for each income group (quintile) given in column 3 and 4 of the table. This shows that if it were a country, India's richest 10 per cent of households would have a per capita GDP rank of around 81 in the world, a total GDP rank of around 19 and a population rank of around 5.

Table 4: Break-up of top 20 per cent (Q5) households

% share of all Indian households

	Income	Expenditure	Surplus income
Richest 10%	36	27	68
Next richest 10%	18	17	24
Total for richest 20% (Q5)	54	44	92

Table 5: Estimated income levels as of 2021–22, as seen through the quintile lens

Income category (% of Indian households)	Average annual household income (Rs lakh)	Total pooled income or 'cumulative income worth' of income group (Rs Billion)	Component of all India GDP resident in each income group or 'GDP worth' of income group ($ billion nominal)*	Per capita per year GDP($) (nominal)
Richest 10%	22	67	1.2	8874
Next 10%	11	34	0.6	4499
Richest 20% (Q5)	16	100	1.8	6687
Next 20% (Q4)	7	41	0.8	2765
Middle 20% (Q3)	4	25	0.4	1632
Next 20 % Quintile 2 (Q2)	2	14	0.3	953
Lowest 20% (Q1)	1	7	0.1	435

* The last two columns have been included to make it easier for people who think in terms of country comparisons. The GDP equivalent of each segment has been computed by taking the income share of each group and multiplying it by the GDP to get the 'GDP share' (nominal GDP, 2021–22, $3.38 trillion). The last column provides the GDP per capita per year of that segment.

Other Methods: Two More Income Classification Schemes to Complete the Library of Household Income Data in India and Comparisons

To illustrate the point made earlier about the many income classifications that exist and get used in India, this section provides two more income classifications in the public domain. Based on ICE 360 data, PRICE, the think tank that conducts the survey, has published its official income classification and the distribution based on that classification. The Boston Consulting Group (BCG) income classification and distribution is popularly used by businesses. PRICE data is based on a primary pan-Indian household survey and details about their methodology are in the public domain. BCG reports are somewhat more economical with details on methodology used but say that their estimates are based on some proprietary surveys and some analogy-based modelling.

I rest my case as far as the use of arbitrary English-language labels for income classification is concerned; clearly, BCG and PRICE have very different ideas of who aspirers are! What is common to both classifications, though, is the large chunk of households lumped into the lower end and the somewhat similar income numbers for the bottom 67 per cent of the income pyramid—clearly, the lower income market is not an area of interest to either.

Table 6 below gives a comparison of income data from both these sources.

Table 6: The ICE 360 official and BCG household income classification and household income distribution versus World Bank-aligned and quintile view of ICE 360 data

ICE 360 official 2020[1]				BCG 2019[2]		
Label	Income range (Rs lakh/year)	% of households		Label	Income range (Rs lakh/year)	% of households
Rich	>30 L	4		Elite	>20 L	3
Strivers	15–30 L	4		Affluent	10–20 L	9
Seekers	5-15 L	25		Aspirers	5–10 L	21
Aspirers	1.25–5 L	52		Next Billion	1.5–5 L	45
Destitutes	< 1.25 L	15		Strugglers	< 1.5 L	22

1. India's Rising Middle-Class Report
Data Source: ICE 360 Survey

2. How India Spends, Shops, Saves report
Data Source: Some proprietary, some analogy-based extrapolation

The next table, Table 7, serves as a ready reference for the average household incomes of all four income classifications and distributions we have discussed in this chapter. There are nuances and differences but the story that runs through all is that the bulk of Indian households have very modest incomes.

Table 7: *Average income per household comparison at a glance*

	World Bank aligned		Quintiles based classification		ICE 360 official report		BCG	
	Percentile band of HH based on HH income	HH Income Rs lakh/year	Percentile	HH Income Rs lakh/year	Percentile	HH Income Rs lakh/year	Percentile	HH Income Rs lakh/year
Highest income	90-100	22	90-100	22	96-100	>30	97-100	>20
					92-96		89-97	15
	70-90	9	80-100	16	67-92	10	69-89	8
			60-80	7				
	50-70	5						
			40-60	4			24-69	3
					15-67	3		
	0-50	2	20-40	2.3				
Lowest income			0-20	1.1	0-15	<1.3	0-24	<1.5

- Way to read percentiles: households have been divided into equal slabs of 1 percent and in terms of their total household income. 90-100 percentile band denotes the richest (highest income) 10% households in India, 0-15 percentile band, the poorest (lowest income) 15% of households, 40-60 percentile band are conceptually are those between the 40th richest household and 60th richest households if all households are taken as 100
- Each percentile point is 3.08M households
- World Bank aligned and quintile based classification analysis done by author using ICE 360 data
- ICE 360 official and BCG classifications available in public domain
- Average incomes for BCG and ICE 360 official data are assumed by me to be the mid point of the ranges rated in their reports. The actual calculated averages may be different

Key Takeaways from Section 1: Understanding Income Structure by Income Group

What are the 'so whats' from this section on the income structure of Consumer India?

First, Indian households are not as rich as we would like them to be and, like it or not, India is a large market comprising a lot of very modest-income households, looking even more modest when converted to US dollars. However, the top 10 per cent of households are where the rich Indian households are, no matter who is counting and how. Even they have a modest per capita income, ranking around 100, relative to the rest of the countries in the world

The richest 20 per cent of households is also where India's middle class lies, based on the mental model most marketers work with. Also, there is a large bottom of the pyramid when measured by global norms, even after so many years of economic growth.

Second, take income classifications with labels that suggest attitudes and behaviour patterns with a large handful of salt, rather than taking them too seriously. That also applies to other labels we see often used in Indian business presentations—for example, 'mass affluent'. They mean different things to different people. Income groups based on percentiles (quintiles) are the clearest way to think about income-based target groups. The income definitions I often hear in most boardroom strategy presentations make me wonder if anyone even knows how exaggerated these numbers are compared to what households actually earn or if the business ambition is limited to the tip of the iceberg of Indian households

Third, when looking at income classes, always keep sight of the percentage of households having that income and the number of households that percentage represents. The more interesting income numbers have very small percentages of households attached to them. But then, in India, a small percentage of a large number is still a large number. As we will see later in the chapter, a relatively large number of households is spread all over the country and not neatly concentrated in pockets.

Finally, as a postscript and a guide to business strategists, please use income data in a quali–quanti manner to reflect on and understand income structures and get a ballpark reality check (a sanity check) on what your consumers actually earn, rather than quibble over the precise numbers and whether they are a year or two old.

SECTION II: Non-income-Based Affluence Classification of Indian Households

NCCS, the Socio-economic Classification System Used by the Market Research Industry

Income is, like paternity, a matter of inference and faith. Consumption is like maternity, a certainty. There is, therefore, a school that believes that ownership of durables and access to select amenities should be the real measure of affluence. The Market Research Society of India (MRSI) has created a non-income, consumption-based classification system of affluence called the NCCS (New Consumer Classification System) using 'ownership' of eleven durables and the education of the chief wage earner. This, in effect, is affluence classification from the consumption side. It correlates well with income, and the affluence classes so defined are discriminating enough in terms of consumer behaviour relating to other items that are not included as variables in the classification system. The list of 'durables' used by the system is electricity connection, ceiling fan, LPG stove, two-wheeler, colour TV, refrigerator, washing machine, PC/laptop, car/jeep/van, air conditioner and agricultural land ownership in rural settings. The classification grades range from A to E (five major classes though the last two are usually combined because of their similar profiles) and within each, there are three sub-classes. So, for example, A1 households are those in which the chief wage earner (CWE) has a graduate or postgraduate or equivalent degree and nine or more durables. The lower social class C2 is a CWE who is literate with up to four years of schooling and a household with 5 durables out of the eleven selected and so on.

There is a wrinkle in defining affluence this way because it has three variables mixed into it—the price of durables, the access to durables finance and the income required to buy them. Mammoth and periodic sales from mega-retailers such as Amazon and the zero or low-interest durable financing offer from Bajaj Finance (where, in effect, the finance company's revenue comes from suppliers having to pay for market access to their large customer base) can and does see durable ownership rise steeply in a very short time even for lower-income groups, thus making this indicator of affluence an unstable one. Kantar Target Group Index (TGI) data shows exactly that. Between 2022 and 2023, the NCCS distribution for households with at least one eighteen to thirty-year-old changed upwards steeply. NCCS A increased by 10 percentage points, NCCS B proportion by 14 per cent, and NCCS D/E proportion dropped by 20 percentage points.

However, durable ownership, when read alongside income data, can offer more insight into how different income levels live.

It is often said that the upper affluence class in India is not as rich as we think they are (and the middle class too, I may add); the lower affluence class is not as poor as we think they are either! The data in Tables 8 (A and B) and 9 reflects that.

Table 8A shows the extent of ownership of select durables by households in each NCCS affluence grade. Table 8B shows the extent of ownership of select durables by households in each income quintile that we discussed in the preceding section.

Table 8A: Ownership of select durables by NCCS grades of affluence

% of households in each group owning

Penetration of durables in each affluence class	Richest 2.5% HH (A1)	Next 5% HH (A2)	Next 10% HH (A3)	Next 10% HH (B1)	Next 12% HH (B2)	Net 15% HH (C1)	Next14 % HH (C2)	Lowest 31% (DE)
Air conditioner	72	30	11	2	<2			
Car	78	32	14	4	<4			
Microwave	44	13	3	L	<1			
Laptop	83	43	19	7	3	<3		
Washing machine	95	68	47	21	7	5	1	<1
Refrigerator	100	97	89	68	44	28	9	<9
Two-wheeler	91	91	88	78	63	46	25	10
Mixer grinder	97	87	76	64	52	42	29	17.8
Inverter	55	33	22	10	5	<5		3
Gas stove	100	100	100	100	100	100	90	76-58

Source: IRS (Indian Readership Survey) 2019 on which the NCCS classification system was developed Data courtesy of MRUC (Media Research Users Council)

Way to read this table: A1 to DE are the affluence grades based on the NCCS system of classification of affluence. The A1 segment is the richest 2.5 per cent of Indian households, 72 per cent of these households have an air conditioner, 78 per cent of these have a car and so on. DE are the poorest 31 per cent of Indian households by this classification system, and 10 per cent of them own a two-wheeler and 18 per cent a mixer grinder and no other durables.

Table 8B: Ownership of select durables by income quintiles

% of households in each group owning

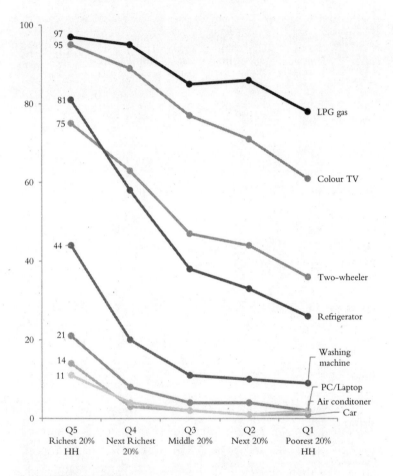

Source: ICE 360 data, 2021

Way to read this table: column two shows that 78 per cent of households among the poorest 20 per cent of Indian households have LPG gas, 36 per cent have a two-wheeler, 26 per cent own a refrigerator (probably second-hand) and so on. The last column has the same data for the richest 20 per cent of Indian households. 81 per cent have refrigerators, 44 per cent have washing machines, just 14 per cent have a car and 11 per cent have an air conditioner. Q1 or quintile 1 are the poorest 20 per cent of households based on household income, Q2 is the next poorest 20 per cent, Q3 is the middle 20 per cent of households stratified based on income, Q4 is the second richest 20 per cent of households and Q5 is the richest 20 per cent of households.

Table 9 gives the ownership of two bundles of durables: a more expensive bundle of car + air conditioners + washing machine + laptop and a less expensive bundle of two-wheeler + refrigerator + colour TV.

Table 9: Household ownership of durables bundles

% of HH Owning each bundle

Segment	Car + Air Con + Washing MC + Laptop/PC	Two-wheeler + Refrigerator + Colour TV
% of Urban HH owning	4.0	52.7
% of Rural HH owning	0.2	28.1
Urban HH owning (million)	4.0	59
Rural HH owning (million)	0.4	55
Indian HH owning (million)	4.4	114
% of NCCS A owning Urban	9	92
(Richest 17.5% HH in India) Rural	1	83

Source: Kantar World Panel 2022

If we apply our mental models of how we think India's rich and middle-income households live (in terms of durables owned), the results are far lower than expected at the top end and better than expected at the middle. Table 9 shows that there are a total of just 4.4 million Indian households that have a car + air conditioners + washing machine + laptop. That is just 1.4 per cent of Indian households, almost entirely in Urban India. On the other hand, there are 114 million households that have a two-wheeler + refrigerator + colour TV. That is 37 per cent of all households, equally distributed in rural and in urban India. This data reminds me of an episode on the popular American serial 'Friends' where one of the female characters says with horror, 'I was so busy trying not to become like my mother that I ended up like my father.' Just as we have been so busy totting up the gains of our premium market, our mass market, spanning both rural and urban India, has bloomed.

Air conditioners, cars and laptops are widely owned only at the very tip of the pyramid, while productivity tools—refrigerators, mixer grinders, two-wheelers and washing machines—have very good penetration across the board. Inverters do well, and the near-universal use of LPG as a cooking medium is possibly a big contributor to Prime Minister Narendra Modi getting the women's vote! Refrigerator penetration is much higher than air conditioner penetration, partly because of the high electricity bills that air conditioners cause and partly because the cost of refrigerators can be offset against money saved in buying larger pack sizes and not wasting food as well as the time saved in daily cooking being used for more earning hours. The latter is a productivity tool, the former is a creature comfort.

The low penetration of high-priced living, comfort-giving durables even at the top of the pyramid can either be interpreted as having 'lots of room for growth', though a fairer interpretation would be that they 'reinforce and reiterate the very low-income numbers'. Growth, however, is pretty much guaranteed as incomes rise over the coming decades, given that all households aspire to all durables that make life more comfortable and more productive, which will in turn enable the household to earn more.

The 'lots of room for growth' interpretation is also valid, but time frames are a question to consider. Venu Srinivasan, the entrepreneur who runs one of India's most iconic two-wheeler companies, TVS Motors, has always maintained that the two-wheeler is to India what the car is to America. The deep penetration of two-wheelers across all social classes (aided by financing, of course) is an indicator of that. Imagine the explosion in the car market in the decades to come as Indian households 'get rich enough' to afford cars. It's perhaps time to start pushing the electric car!

Chart 2: Absolute income levels by quintile over time

The COVID effect: Observed versus expected

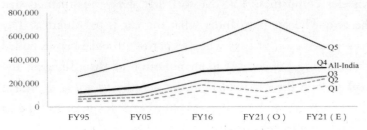

Annual average household income (Rs at 2011–12 prices)

Q1: Lower 20% | Q2: Second Lower 20% | Q3: Middle 20% | Q4: Next richest 20%
Q5: Richest 20%

Table 10: Trends in share of income by different quintiles, 1994–2021

% share of all India household income in each income quintile

Year of survey data	1994–1995	2004–2005	2015–2016	FY21 Estimated based on past trends	FY21 Actual income observed in the 2021 survey	Gain/ loss in income share of quintile Observed vs Actual
Lowest 20% Q1	5.9	5.2	7.0	7.8	3.3	-4.5
Second lowest 20% Q2	9.6	8.7	10.9	11.8	7.2	-4.6
Middle 20% Q3	13.6	12.8	15.2	16.1	12.3	-3.8
Second richest 20% Q4	20.7	20.6	22.1	22.4	20.9	-1.5
Richest 20% Q5	50.2	52.7	44.9	41.8	56.3	+14.5
All Indian households	100.0	100	100	100	100	

(Quintiles of population based on per capita income)

Source: 1995 data from 'The Well Being of Indian Households', NCAER and TMH; 2005 data from 'How India Earns, Spends and Saves', NCAER and Sage; 2014, 2016, 2021 data from ICE 360 survey, waves 1, 2, 3.
*Data pertains to 1994–95, 2004–05, 2015–16, 2020–21 April to March. Estimates projected by PRICE analysts.
Way to read this table: Column 2 shows that in the year 1994–95, the lowest income quintile had 5.9% of all Indian household income. Column 3 shows that this became 5.2% in the year 2004–05, and column 4 shows that it became 7.0% in the year 2015–16. Projecting this trend, column 5 shows that this lowest income group should have had 7.8% of all Indian household income. However, as column 7 shows, the survey data showed that the actual share of income of this group dropped to 3.3%. The remaining rows apply to the remaining quintiles.

Section III: Trends in Income Distribution and COVID Impact

Chart 2 depicts the absolute income levels for each quintile from 1995 till 2021, wherever survey data points are available. FY 2016 was the last surveyed data point before FY 21. In the intervening years between FY 2019 and FY 2020, real GDP growth had slowed down to 4.5 per cent and 3.7 per cent. In 2020–21, on account of the lockdowns caused by the pandemic, real GDP declined by 6.6 per cent. Therefore, it is a good indicator of what happens to income during times of economic stress.

FY 2021(O) is the observed level of income as obtained from the survey. FY 2021(E) is the expected level of income based on projecting past rates of growth of incomes in every quintile, based on data from 1994 onwards. This also includes the periods of very good economic growth 2003–10, except for 2008. As Chart 2 shows, the observed levels of income of the richest 20 per cent were far higher than the expected, forecast levels and the reverse occurred for the poorest quintile, where the observed levels were far lower than the ones forecast.

Table 10, the companion table to the chart, shows the share of income that each quintile has between 1994–95 and 2021 and also the observed versus the expected share of income in 2021 of each quintile.

Over the decades, the share of income 'captured' or contained in the richest 20 per cent of households was decreasing, and data showed that a 'trickle down' was happening. Table 10 shows that the richest 20 per cent of households (Q5) had 50.2 per cent of India's household income in 1994–95, which steadily decreased to 44.9 per cent in 2016. Had this trend continued, the income share of the top 20 per cent richest households would have further decreased to 41.8 per cent (see second last column of the table). However, the two years of slowdown in economic growth preceding the pandemic followed by the COVID years have battered the lower income groups, while the uppermost quintile has been a big gainer.

This is also seen in the third companion table, Table 11 below, which gives the surplus income to the total income ratio for every income quintile in 2021 compared to 2016. While the surplus income ratio has expectedly declined for all households, the lower three quintiles have seen their surplus incomes collapse and turn negative/more negative. The richest 20 per cent have seen their surplus ratios declining only slightly, and the next richest 20 per cent have seen their surplus income to total income ratio drop by 35 per cent but still remain positive.

The Resilience of the Richest 20 Per Cent of Households

Tables 10 and 11 together show that the richest 20 per cent (Q5) of households have increased their share of income during the pandemic period because this group has the highest skills and education relative to the rest. As a result, they presumably had a much better ability to work remotely. 38 per cent of CWEs in Q5 have tech or vocational or graduate degrees and beyond in the richest 20 per cent of households as compared to 7 per cent in Q2, the lower middle or second poorest 20 per cent slab of households. Q5 has also had, consistently over time, almost all of the surplus income of Indian households, giving it staying power in bad times. Because many of the CWEs have regular salaried jobs or are self-employed in agriculture with above average land holdings, they have continued to earn during the

Table 11: Surplus income to total income ratio, pre- and post-slowdown and COVID

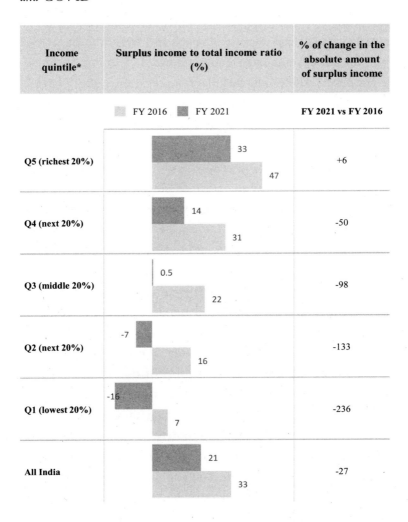

Income quintile*	Surplus income to total income ratio (%)		% of change in the absolute amount of surplus income
	FY 2016	FY 2021	FY 2021 vs FY 2016
Q5 (richest 20%)		33 / 47	+6
Q4 (next 20%)		14 / 31	-50
Q3 (middle 20%)		0.5 / 22	-98
Q2 (next 20%)		-7 / 16	-133
Q1 (lowest 20%)		-16 / 7	-236
All India		21 / 33	-27

Source: ICE 360 survey * Population quintiles based on per capital income

Way to read this table: Row relating to Q5: Column 2 shows that Q5 had a surplus income to total income ratio of 47% in FY 2016 and Column 3 shows that post COVID, the surplus income to total income ratio dropped to 33%. However, as column 4 shows, the absolute amounts of surplus income went up by 6% (even if the ratio to the total income went down). The remaining rows relate to the rest of the household income quintiles.

pandemic years of lockdowns and curtailed movement, unlike
the lower income groups—such as casual labour or petty service
providers—who cannot work remotely. As much as 67 per cent
of those in Q5, the richest 20 per cent, have regular salaried
jobs or are self-employed in agriculture, i.e., doing farming as
a business. Detailed discussion on occupation follows later in
these chapters on the structure story.

The so-called K-shaped performance that we have seen in
the case of companies (where there is one group that does very
well and one that does very badly) seems to apply to people too.
Strong companies have got stronger in the pandemic, gaining
market share and, in certain categories, enjoying a sharp increase
in consumer demand (for example, certain categories of food
and food service, information and communications technology
[ICT] equipment for an online world, online entertainment,
stock trading etc.), which has resulted in a higher 'new normal'
as compared to business-as-usual trends. Weak companies, on
the other hand, have been debilitated to varying degrees—
some have died, others have lost a lot of capabilities, assets and
linkages and will take varying degrees of time before they get
back on the growth track. Since such small companies do not
have retained earnings over the years large enough to give them
staying power and both they and lenders are cautious with loans,
their situation worsens. Small companies have fallen into both
buckets—those who have managed to prune portfolios or pivot
to new business lines and embrace e-commerce and those who
have not been able to change for the new world.

Similarly, the K-shaped recovery has happened to Consumer
India as well. The upper half is doing well, even better in the
uppermost quintile. The trends of high price-performance points
(premium categories) doing well, travel, food service doing

well, iPhones and cars doing well, and agriculture not being too disrupted (beyond its usual woes) are likely to continue for reasons discussed. Mass market incomes are almost entirely from the informal sector, dependent on agriculture and construction and non-financial services like transport and logistics, hospitality etc., and they are vulnerable.

Future Income Distribution Pattern: Will It Go Back to a Less Top-Heavy, Less Unequal Distribution?

This severely skewed income share of the richest 20 per cent of households (Q5) having a whopping 56 per cent share of all of India's household income is the result of the pandemic years, which preceded the economic slowdown in FY 2019 and FY 2020. Between FY 2019 and FY 2020, pre-pandemic, real GDP growth had slowed to 4.5 per cent and 3.7 per cent; in FY 2021, on account of COVID disruptions, real GDP declined -6.6 per cent and recovered to 8.7 per cent in FY 2022, though from a smaller base, and the recovery was sustained at a 7.0 per cent in FY 2023. The question is, will the income distribution come back to the less skewed, pre-pandemic structure as the economy recovers further, now that Consumer India is back to its day-to-day life and migrant workers from the villages have mostly returned to their urban places of work? We do not have data to predict this, and I do not have the confidence to do so, but here's an assessment of what may be the case based on what we see on the ground.

When the economy does really well—measured not just by a single GDP number but by the underlying nature of increased economic activity across the board and increased investment across a wide range of sectors—the tide rises, and everyone does well. It is de rigueur in the Indian discourse on consumption, often fashionable, especially with impatient TV anchors, to think about consumption in isolation as an autonomous variable, divorced and siloed from either investment or the nature of supply available. The simple fact, however, is that consumption is linked to both.

I am often asked by TV anchors to comment on what is happening with consumption, why it is slowing down or what can be done to boost it. When I say, in response, that people need to earn in order to spend and they will earn more if the economy hums and work gets created all around, I can see the look in their eyes that says, 'Interrupt her, she is wandering off the brief.' I try to explain to them that when investment kick-starts the economy into a higher gear, more trucks will move with goods from factories to markets, and truck drivers, truck cleaners, dhabawaalas (owners of roadside eateries), chicken suppliers to the dhabas and even Chhotu who cleans tables will all earn more. Given this, can we talk about how we can make more investment pick-up? I am usually firmly shut down and told, 'But today, on this show, we are discussing consumption.'

Table 12 has the data on the share of income that each income group had in 2015–16 and for 2020–21. The 2015–16 income distribution shows what a period of strong economic growth can produce in terms of trickle-down of income and can perhaps be considered as the outer bound of how good it can get in the medium term, from where it is now. The share of the richest 20 per cent of households could drop to less than half and its share of surplus income could drop from 92 per cent to 70 per cent with the gainers in income share being Q3 (middle 20 per cent), Q2 and Q1 (40 per cent, comprising the lowest income quintile and one level above that). More reassuring

Table 12: Income distribution after good times and bad times

Population quintiles based on per capita income	Pre-pandemic (2015–16): After the good years		Post-pandemic and slowdown (2020–21): After the bad years	
	Share of total household income captured by quintile %	Share of total household surplus income captured by quintile %	Share of total household income captured by quintile %	Share of total household surplus income captured by quintile%
Richest 20% Q5	45	70	54	92
Next 20% Q4	22	22	22	14
Middle 20% Q3	15	9	13	0
Next 20% Q2	11	3	8	-4
Poorest 20% Q1	7	-3	3	-2

Source : ICE 360 data

Average annual growth rate (AAGR percentage) of real GDP across financial years 2004 to 2016

2004	2005	2006	2007	2008	2009	2010	2011	2012	2013	2014	2015	2016
7.92	7.92	8.06	7.66	3.09	7.86	8.50	5.24	5.46	6.39	7.40	8.00	8.26

is the distribution of surplus income. Q4 (the second richest 20 per cent of households) and Q3 (the middle 20 per cent) are the biggest gainers in surplus income share and that will boost consumption of durables and discretionary experiences. Q4 becomes exceptionally stronger, with the ability to retain its share of income in good and bad times and hence all further income growths become surplus income. We are already seeing that anecdotally, between 2021 and today.

In sum, it is good news for most companies that the top of the income pyramid has gained a greater share of income (though regrettable from a human point of view), and the positive effect of this has been visible in the financial performance of a certain set of good companies whose target market is the richest 20 per cent. We will see premium markets grow faster as suppliers put more effort into them, going after where the money is. In any case, most of the large companies in India are not seriously targeting consumers below that level except as a spillover driven by small packs and wholesale distribution.

The exceptions are a few large players, such as Jio telecom and entertainment services, HUL (turnover Rs 503 billion, net profit 881 billion) and ITC for the cigarette business (Rs 234 billion annual turnover), who have demonstrated that there is indeed fortune at the bottom of the pyramid and shown what size a truly mass-market business can be. For example, Reliance Industries-owned streaming platform Jio Cinema is streaming the Tata IPL for free on the OTT platform. Viacom18, a part of the Reliance Group, bought IPL's streaming rights for $2.7 billion for 2023–27. The viewership was staggering at almost 1.5 billion video views, with 57 minutes on average being spent by each viewer. Jio is monetizing this service through advertising and also by way of jump-starting Jio Cinema, a Netflix competitor with original content.

Section IV: Understanding Income Structure by Education, Occupation and Geographic Profiles of Income Group

A Deeper Dive into Profiles of the Top Two Income Quintiles of Households

As has been said earlier, most large businesses, with a handful of exceptions, target the richest 20 per cent of households, and think about them as India's rising 'middle class'. In terms of pain and gain, this is a good segment, more so as we just discussed, in the post-COVID era where the rich got significantly richer. Tables 13A, 13B and 13C provide a deep dive into this group in terms of where they live, how they earn their money and what education level they have. There are surprises here that call for mental model adjustment and for re-examining 'doesn't everyone know, it's obvious' wisdom.

The next richest 20 per cent is the next logical segment that companies look towards for business growth, especially as incomes rise with each year. As we have seen in the previous section, this segment is poised to capture an increased share of incremental growth in national income as a result of GDP growth. Tables 13A, 13B and 13C provide a deep dive into the profile of this segment as well.

When widening the consumer net, the question that companies should be asking themselves (but usually do not) is: how similar are the households in this second richest 20 per cent segment (Quintile 4 or Q4) to those in the richest 20 per cent group (Quintile 5 or Q5) that has been their core target consumer so far. Tables 13A, 13B and 13C show the difference between the two segments and what the combined consumer profile would look like when both segments are to be served with equal intensity. This is a helpful analysis because as the data will show, companies will need to adjust their market strategy when expanding from serving the richest 20 per cent to serving the wider swathe of the richest 40 per cent of Indian households.

Table 13A: Location profile of the richest 40 per cent of Indian households (Q5 and Q4)

Income group	Rich 20% Q5	Next 20% Q4	Combined Top 40% Q5+Q4
LOCATION			
Metro	22	8	15
Tier 1 towns	10	10	10
Tier 2 towns	11	12	12
Rest of urban	12	10	11
Total Urban	**55**	**40**	**48**
Development rural	17	11	14
Emerging rural	16	18	17
Underdeveloped rural	12	31	22
Total Rural	**45**	**60**	**53**
Total	**100**	**100**	**100**

Table 13B: Occupation profile of the richest 40 per cent of Indian households (Q5 and Q4)

% of each quintile dependent on each occupation

Profile item	Rich 20% Q5	Next 20% Q4	Combined top 40% Q5+Q4
Occupation of CWE			
Own agriculture business	17	23	20
Regular salary/wage—public	17	7	12
Regular salary/wage—private	33	22	27
Own business—non-agricultural	17	16	17
Wage labour—agricultural/allied	1	5	3
Wage labour—non-agricultural	2	15	18
Retired/Pension/Rent on properties etc.	10	9	
Total	**100**	**100**	**100**

Table 13C: Education profile of the richest 40 per cent of Indian households (Q5 and Q4)

% of each quintile with CWE at each education level

Profile item	Rich 20% Q5	Next 20% Q4	Combined top 40%
Education of CWE			
Low or no literacy/no schooling	11	18	14
Some schooling	23	37	29
Finished school (class 10/11/12)	37	36	36
Technical/Diploma	9	2	5
Graduate	23	7	11
Postgraduate and professional	6	1	3
Total	**100**	**100**	**100**

Profile of richest 20 per cent and the need to recalibrate many popular assumptions

Where are they? The popular assumption that many business strategists hold is that the rich live in metros and large towns while the poor live in villages. This is absolutely not true. About half of the richest 20 per cent of households is evenly spread across rural India. As much as 17 per cent of this group are in the agricultural business, most likely owners of large tracts of land and enjoying the benefits of non-taxable agricultural income. Only 22 per cent live in metros.

This pattern of rich households being well spread across all tiers of towns and villages is true even for the super-rich 10 million households.[4] While 50 per cent of this category is estimated to be in metros (theoretical distribution, not survey distribution), 28 per cent are in peri-urban or semi-rural areas (villages adjoining large towns or small towns adjoining large villages), and 19 per cent are in tier-2 towns (population 1–5 million).

Therefore, even to serve just the rich households, marketers will still need to have an all-India distribution. The success of the Korean durables company LG in India has been its ability to identify pools of moneyed households in every part of India and access them and mop them up cost-effectively.

How do they earn? The fragility of income of even the star consumer classes in Consumer India is evident from the occupation of the chief wage earner (Table 13 B). The faulty mental models of many businesses, especially financial services, when they say their target group is 'salaried, graduates' is apparent from this data.

Only 50 per cent of households in the richest 20 per cent group of households get a regular salary, 34 per cent have a self-employed chief wage earner—17 per cent in the business of agriculture and 17 per cent non-agricultural, both subject to a lot of income volatility built into the nature of their occupation, even though, arguably, agriculture is more volatile given that rain is a less controllable variable.

To be honest, while these labels of occupation type are truthful, more accurately, those owning farming businesses usually have small land holdings. Here's a rough-and-ready calculation—0.6 per cent of India's farmers have land holdings above 10 hectares, and another 13 per cent between 2 and 10 hectares. This group comprises the richest 8 per cent of India's farmers. Similarly, over 99 per cent of India's businesses are micro-enterprises, with investments of less than Rs 1 crore and turnover of less than Rs 5 crore. Just 1 per cent of businesses are medium or large. This group has about 7 per cent of households dependent on their own business, which means many of them are micro businesses, assuming one business per household.

As much as 20 per cent of households in the second richest 20 per cent are dependent on some form of casual labour, presumably skilled enough to enable them to earn enough to get into this bracket.

How educated are they? India's education system needs a huge upgrade and much has been written about this. While there is improvement in each successive generation, the overall picture continues to be bleak. A third of the chief wage earners of even the richest 20 per cent of Indian households have not even finished school while another 30 per cent have a college education and another 9 per cent have technical (polytechnic diploma type) education.

This is a very heterogeneous group in terms of occupation, begging the thought that social class that transcends income should be the basis for deciding target markets.

So clearly, the takeaway from occupation and education profiles of the richest 20 per cent of households is that there is a great deal of heterogeneity in how rich households earn, begging the thought that social class that transcends income should be the basis for deciding target markets in India or there needs to be a more segmented market game even to target just the top of the income pyramid. This heterogeneity gets even more pronounced once the target market is defined as the top 40 per cent of Indian households by income, as the section below shows, as does the data in Table 13 (A, B and C).

Difference in the profile of the second richest 20 per cent of households compared to the richest 20 per cent

The profile 'drops' significantly between the two segments of households that form the mainstay of Indian household income and surplus income and represent the target universe group for several companies. The second richest 20 per cent is more rural and far less present in metros (see table 13A) and has a 'poorer' occupational profile of almost 40 per cent agricultural (23 per cent agricultural business and 15 per cent wage labour in agriculture). In terms of education, over 50 per cent of these households have no one who has finished school (see tables 13B and 13C).

'Lazy marketing' needs to rethink its assumptions, accept the reality and work with it

The idea of this discussion is to debunk the notion that it is metro, large-town, executive-type, salaried, well-educated people who are driving India's consumption. Rather, this conceptualization is of a small, easily accessible pool of households that lazy marketers would like to focus on. By this definition, only 40 per cent of the top quintile of households and 10–30 per cent of the next quintile of households would qualify. That means that of the 62 million households in this group that they think they are targeting, by this definition, they only target half of them—25 million Q5 households and 6 million Q4 households.

Income Structure by Geographic Segments of Town Class (Urban/Rural and Size of Towns)

This section addresses the following questions:

(i)   How much total or pooled income, expenditure and surplus resides in or is contained in different sizes of towns and village clusters by development levels? This is a very useful reality check for those who believe that metros have it all or that metros and tier-2 towns make up almost the entire income pie.

(ii) What is the income profile of each geographic cluster or segment? The previous section asked and answered 'What is the geographic profile of the richest two income groups'.

(i) *Income, expenditure and surplus distribution across different sizes of towns and village clusters by development levels*

Table 14: Share of all-India household income, expenditure and surplus income across geographic strata

% share in each geographic stratum

Geographic segment	Households	Income	Expenditure	Surplus income	Population share to income share INDEX
Metros[6]	9	18	15	27	2.0
Tier 1[7]	8	9	9		1.1
Tier-2 or niche cities	8	10	10	8	1.1
Rest of urban or census towns	12	11	12	9	1.0
All urban	**36**	**47**	**45**	**54**	**1.3**
Developed rural[8]	9	14	12	18	1.5
Emerging rural	23	18	19	15	0.8
Under-developed rural	32	21	24	13	0.7
All rural	**64**	**53**	**55**	**46.0**	**0.83**
Total	**100**	**100**	**100**	**100**	

Source: ICE 360 data

Way to read the table: Metros have 9 per cent of India's households, 18 per cent of Indian household income, 15 per cent of India's household expenditure and 27 per cent share of surplus income of Indian households.

The last column is an indicator of how much above or below the population share the income share of each cluster is. A value of 1.0 would mean that the income share is in line with the occupation share for any cluster. Above 1.0 means that this geographic cluster holds more income than its population weight entitles it to, and less than 1.0 means that it contains less income than its population weight entitles it to. The value of 2.0 for metros shows metros are punching at double their population weight, while underdeveloped rural at 0.7 shows it is punching at just two-thirds of their population weight.

This data in Table 14 reiterates what has been discussed earlier in this chapter—income, expenditure and surplus income are well distributed across the country. A business that addresses a target market of the top sixty-three towns in India—effectively consumers resident only in metros and large towns, i.e., tier 1 and 2 towns—will only address 36 per cent of India's income and less than half of the surplus income of Consumer India. Add to that a skimming rural strategy of just 'developed rural', which are typically rural areas adjoining large cities, and the addressed market will be about half of India's household income and 62 per cent of surplus income. What's more, it will offer very rich and fertile soil because of its relative concentration of affluence in these pockets, as seen in the population-to-income ratio. The excitement of the last decade has been about the demonstrated consumption growth in smaller towns (loosely called tier 2 towns by marketers and media and in this table called tier 1 and tier 2 towns based on size and a few other characteristics). It is often incorrectly assumed that this consumption growth in smaller towns represents an increased consumption from less affluent people because it is assumed (legacy thinking) that money resides in the big towns. That was true pre-1991, but not any more. In the age of rapidly expanding road, rail and air networks and then Internet ubiquitousness and very low telecom rates, the lower cost of living in smaller towns motivated many businesses to expand to smaller towns (especially IT services delivery centres employing large numbers of young people), colleges have mushroomed in smaller towns as has the start-up ecosystem; business owners in smaller towns have been able to expand their footprint including their physical footprint without actually moving to larger cities.

That said, the 'underdeveloped rural', which comprises a very large chunk of around one-third of India's population and about 100 million Indian households in the least developed districts of India, punches way below its weight in terms of income yet collectively holds more income than the metros (though half of its surplus income). Also, the sheer weight of remote rural and small-town, less-affluent Consumer India in India's domestic consumption story is clear from this data. Their growth because of large numbers and low bases will also be significant.

Companies that were late to embrace small towns and rural markets but are doing so now with a big push are growing much faster than their peers, as they tap into new well-off consumer pools. Erroneously, stock market analysts mistake this spurt for a sudden resurgence of macro consumer demand—especially if the company is a market leader, their growth will show up in aggregate industry growth and further confuse analysts with simplistic models!

(ii) *Income profile of each geographic cluster*

The preceding section and Table 14 have just discussed the question of how much pooled income is resident in each geographical cluster given how many people it has and their income distribution. Table 15 provides insight into the income distribution in each geographic stratum i.e. out of 100 households in any stratum, how many belong to Q5 (are amongst the richest 20 per cent of Indian households), Q4 and so on.

Table 15: Relative income levels across geographic strata

Geographic strata	Index of average household income	% share of each all-India quintile present in each geography					
		Q5[1]	Q4	Q3	Q2	Q1	Total
Metros	100	53	19	14	9	6	100
Tier 1	55	25	26	13	18	17	100
Tier 2	55	25	29	15	18	13	100
Rest of urban	46	20	18	18	19	25	100
Developed rural	71	38	23	14	14	11	100
Emerging rural	38	14	16	25	22	22	100
Underdeveloped rural	32	7	19	23	25	25	100

1. Q5 is the richest 20 per cent of Indian households, while Q1 is the poorest 20 per cent of Indian households.

Way to read the table: Column 2 shows that if the average household income in a metro is indexed to 100, then the average household in Tier 1 and 2 cities earns 55, the average household in other urban towns earns 46 and so on. Row 2 shows that in metros. 53% of all households living there belong to India's richest 20% households (Q5)and only 6 per cent the poorest 20 (Q1). In the last row, underdeveloped rural, 7 per cent of households resident here are in the richest 20% of Indian households (Q5), but 25 per cent are in the poorest 20% (Q1).

Interestingly, excluding the metros, the rest of large- *and* small-town urban India has similar income profiles, yet again reinforcing the point that income is scattered all over India.

Developed rural areas continue to outshine tier 1 and 2 towns in their income profile, and households in underdeveloped rural areas have the lowest income relative to metro households as well as the poorest income distribution, with half of their households belonging to the poorest 50 per cent of Indian households.

The data also shows that, while it is correct to say that most of India's lowest-income households live in rural India, it is also correct to say that almost half of India's rich households also live in rural India, as we have just seen.

The great Indian number trick is visible in Tables 14 and 15 read together. Underdeveloped rural areas have almost one-third of India's households, each of which has a third of the income of a metro household; 50 per cent of this geographic segment is in the poorest two quintiles, and yet this section collectively has 20 per cent higher total income and 53 per cent higher total expenditure than the metros, 50 per cent of whose residents are in the richest 20 per cent of segment of India.

The Structure Story of Urban-Rural

Reiterating the importance of rural India and trends in rural-urban income shares

Rural India plays a major role in India's consumer demand, as the last section has also shown. The old conceptualization of 'India' (urban) and 'Bharat' (rural)—mapping precisely on to rich and poor, educated and not, having modern amenities and left behind in the dark ages, wearing trousers and wearing

pyjamas—doesn't work as precisely any more. There are shades
and grades of rural India based on access to amenities, education,
economic activity and diversification out of agriculture to other
occupations. The gap in development between rural and urban
areas has also narrowed.

Table 16: Importance of rural India in India's consumption

Relative share of urban/rural India on each parameter

Location	Number of households (million)	Share of households %	Share of income %	Share of expenditure %	Share of surplus income %	Rural average household income relative to urban
■ Urban	111	36	47	45	54	100
▦ Rural	197	64	53	55	46	56
All-India	308	100	100	100	100	72

Ignore rural India and about half of India's household
consumption is ignored. However, it's the usual maths we
see in India—a larger number of relatively poorer households
collectively adding up to more income and consumption than a
smaller number of more affluent people.

Table 17: Trends in the rural share of each income group (2016–21)

Population quintiles based on per capita income	2016 Rural - Urban	2021 Rural - Urban
Richest 20% (Q5)	56 / 44	52 / 48
Next richest 20% (Q4)	42 / 58	38 / 62
Middle 20% (Q3)	30 / 70	26 / 74
Next 20% (Q2)	18 / 82	29 / 71
Poorest 20% (Q1)	11 / 89	31 / 69
All India	34 / 66	36 / 64

Rural ▦ Urban

Way to read this table: Row 2 shows that India's Q5 households in 2016 were 44 per cent in rural India and 56 per cent in urban India. In 2021, India's Q5 households were 48 per cent in rural India and 52 per cent in urban India. Row 6 shows that India's Q1 households were 89 per cent in rural India and 11 per cent in urban India in 2016. In 2021, they were 69 per cent in rural India and 36 per cent in urban India.

Table 17 shows that between 2016 and 2021 (which includes the COVID years), rural India has been increasing its share of rich households and decreasing its share of low-income households. Urban 'poverty' is also clearly visible from this data. the share of urban India in the poorest 20 per cent of households has increased from 11 per cent to 31 per cent. It is possible that this is the COVID effect, where urban areas were hit worse than rural.

The blurring urban-rural divide and the need for a new, more sensible definition of urbanization that reflects reality

As discussed in the preceding sections of this chapter, the urban–rural continuum is blurred, and village-like census towns and tier 1 and 2 city-like 'developed rural' pockets are examples of this blur.

The reasons for this continuous blurring (and even more to come) lie in the way India defines 'rural' and 'urban'. This understanding will contribute far more insight into Consumer India's rural–urban structure than will the tracking of statistics on urbanization.

India defines 'rural' as anything that is not 'urban'. A settlement is called urban if it qualifies on four counts—it is governed by a local urban body, has a population of over 5000, has 75 per cent of its male population not engaged in agriculture and has a population density of 400 people per square kilometre. Census towns qualify on other criteria but are governed by the village system of panchayats.

Shamika Ravi, of the Economic Advisory Council to the Prime Minister (EAC-PM) writes in a March 2023 working paper titled 'What is Urban/Rural India' that 'the current classification criteria are often inadequate to capture the scale and speed of urbanisation'.

Census towns, which are what marketers refer to as 'semi-urban' or 'peri-urban', number up to almost 4000. They have obtained urban characteristics but are not administered as other urban towns are, instead being governed as villages are by panchayats. They have a large governance deficit, being as they are in no man's land. 'Developed' rural areas on the other hand are a jewel in the rural portfolio—a village technically, they typically adjoin large towns and have the income levels between tier 1 towns and metros and almost the same number of households as metros.

An article in *Mint* by Ajai Sreevatsan, 'How much of India is actually urban'[8] says that if we examine satellite image data about built-up areas, we find that 63 per cent of India is urban and not 31 per cent, as the census 2011 says (or 34 per cent now, as per commonly accepted projection). He argues that another way to see this is that if all settlements with more than 5000 people were considered to be urban with no further criteria, then the urban population of India would be 47 per cent of the total population. He suggests that if a correlation is evaluated between the share of urban population and per capita incomes, the satellite imaging definition fails the test, but the definition of 5000 or more inhabitants does as well as the existing definition of the census. His conclusion is pretty much what marketers' experiences of the last decade have been—there is a rural–urban continuum, and thinking about it this way is perhaps more useful than what he calls a 'rural/urban binary'. Much of urban India's growth, according to the Centre for Policy Research data, is due to 'organic' reasons for more births in urban India and due to the reclassification of villages as towns rather than people migrating from rural areas to urban areas.

Other factors that contribute to the blurring of the urban-rural divide

Urbanization is supposed to offer large-scale opportunities for formal and more value-added occupations for people who are coming out of farming, as has happened in several countries, most notably China. It is also supposed to provide access to better public goods and amenities to enable people to better take advantage of available opportunities for better work.

The similar informality of occupations in both urban and rural India for the lower income groups and the similar lack of access to amenities that change the way they live—easy public transport and 24/7 and in-home availability of water etc.—are contributing to the lack of stark differences between urban and rural areas, especially in non-metros.

Table 18: Nature of rural and urban occupations

Occupation of Chief Wage Earner (CWE)	% of households in rural/urban dependent on each occupation	
	Rural India	Urban India
Self-employed in agriculture (farm owner/renter/agri business)	48	-
Self-employed in non-agriculture	11	39
Total self-employed	59	39
Total casual labour	27	14
Regular wage/salary (mostly informal)	14	47

Source: NSS Annual Report Periodic Labour Force Survey July 2022–June 2023

Table 18, based on the National Sample Survey periodic labour force study, shows the similarity of occupations in both urban and rural India, contradicting conventional wisdom that urbanization generally creates more value-added jobs. 48 per cent of all rural household CWEs are self-employed in agriculture, which means that they are mostly marginal farmers, and 39 per cent of all urban household CWEs are self-employed in non-agricultural occupations, which means that they mostly have micro-enterprises,[9] which have the same degree of instability and precarious profitability as marginal farmers. While it appears from Table 18 that a much higher proportion of households are salaried in urban India as compared to rural India (47 per cent versus 14 per cent, respectively), most of them are actually informal workers. Seventy per cent do not have a written contract, and over half do not have paid leave or social security. Besides, many of them are working for informal enterprises.

Just 22 per cent of the workforce in urban India work in manufacturing as compared to 8 per cent in rural India, and 50 per cent of workers in urban areas are in low-paid jobs in services. Later chapters will discuss the exact nature of occupation in India, but for now, between rural occupation profiles and urban ones, there is no evidence that urbanization creates better quality, more secure jobs, and hence is better for the future of consumption.

The other factors that cause the blurring between rural and urban are the improved access that rural India has to urban consumer goods and services and the near-identical entertainment and social media. Road connectivity, thanks to the village roads programme of the government, has bridged the distance between the nearest small town and also bridged the cultural and lifestyle distance between the two. Additionally, digital reach enables the same television programmes, the same ubiquitous WhatsApp with its humour mill, friend groups and internet access. Of course, there are differences in the delivered quality of digital services between villages and towns, but often, I get better signals on roads in remote interior India than I do in my Mumbai apartment or some office buildings. The point is that everyone in India now knows what is possible and where to access it.

We will talk more about this in a later chapter, but start-ups, now unicorns, like ShareChat, are designed to be the small town/rural person's social media and are tailor-made for them.

Mass Markets of Scale at Last: The Outcome of Income and Connectivity Similarities

For all these reasons of blurring minds and wallets and lifestyles, it is reasonable and perhaps more appropriate to conceive of some segments of urban and rural Consumer India as a single market, albeit with a few executional go-to-market differences and operational inefficiencies. This finally gives Indian marketers an enormous scale for the first time, especially for mass marketers.

Chart 3 shows the structure of Consumer India in terms of similar-income households that can be viewed as a single market. In each income segment, the proportion of urban and rural varies as the table shows.

There is a mass market that in India we euphemistically call the 'popular' (those who can only afford lower price-performance products) segment of 100–120 million households equally distributed between rural and urban areas, earning between Rs 1 lakh and Rs 3 lakh a year and another segment more affluent that I will label 'high end popular' of 55–85 million households earning between Rs 4 lakh to Rs 8 lakh a year, also equally distributed between rural and urban.

There are two segments above this with varying degrees of affluence, which are in majority urban but have a significant rural component. They are a group of around 25 million households in the Rs 10 lakh to Rs 15 lakh band, another 10 million or so households in the Rs 18 lakh to Rs 20 lakh annual income bracket, and a third super-premium segment of about 2 million households, also equally urban and rural, interestingly.

As access to amenities and public goods improves in rural India, the boundary will get even blurrier, and the combined markets even more interesting. India has over 6,00,000 villages, with 20,000 of them having 40 per cent of the rural population as per the 2011 census, and we await the new decadal census.

Logistically speaking, rural India is of course more scattered geographically, but accessibility is increasing and transport is getting cheaper by the day given the very vibrant logistics and distribution services coming up in order to serve e-commerce. Also contributing to greater accessibility is the ubiquitousness of digital payments and the high-intensity start-up activity to connect rural markets and urban supply and vice versa, which we will elaborate on in the last chapter.

Government statistics show steady improvement in access to amenities such as electricity and drinking water—most villages have them now, even though they have not reached all homes yet; every unit of infrastructure and amenities improvement will drive consumption, as will every unit of increase in income.

Chart 3: Grouping of households with similar income—across rural and urban India

Mass markets at last spanning Urban + Rural

Income Rs lakhs/year	Rural HH 197 mn	Urban HH 111mn	Total HH (mn)
25+			2.2
20 to 25			0.0
18 to 20			8.4
12 to 15			12.9
10 to 12			12.9
8 to 10			12.3
6 to 8			25.2
4 to 6			55.4
3 to 4			28.6
2 to 3			43.1
1 to 2			67.2
0.5 to 1			16.2
<0.5			6.2

Way to read this chart: The number of households in rural and urban India has been plotted at each level of average annual household income. The first column on the left is the household income level, and the last column on the right is the number of households spanning both urban and rural that have the corresponding income level. and the bar chart in the middle shows how the group of households with this average income is distributed between urban and rural Indian households. In the highest income group of average income of Rs 25 lakh and above (first column), there are 2.24 million households (right column), and they are slightly more urban but with a significant rural component. At an income level of Rs 1–2 lakh per annum, there are 67.2 million households almost equally divided between urban and rural.

How Consumer India Earns: The Structure Story of Occupation and Education

Occupation structure of Consumer India

The one big fly in the ointment in the consumption story of India is the occupation structure. The fact that the source of income for most households is non-formal and not based on a regular salary makes for income and consumption volatility and a great deal of fragility when faced with economic shocks.

In several places in this chapter, this point has been made using occupation data. To bring the point home, Table 19 presents occupation data at a glance for all of India, categorized by income classes.

Table 19: Occupation profile of Consumer India as a whole and share of income expenditure and surplus income captured by each occupation group

% share of all-India households in each occupation group

Main source of income (occupation of CWE)	Share of households %	Share of income %	Share of expenditure %	Share of surplus income %
Self-employed in agriculture	20	19	18	25
Petty traders (no permanent establishment)	2	2	2	0
Shop owners/businessmen (with permanent establishment)	8	12	12	12
Self-employed non-professional	1	1	1	1
Grade 4 employees (services providing help in household and commercial establishments, usually informally employed but salaried)	12	17	17	17
Clerical (usually formally employed but junior)	5	8	7	12
Supervisory level (usually formally employed)	3	7	5	11
Officer (usually formerly employed senior-level help)	2	6	5	10
Self employed professional	3	3	3	2
Labour (agricultural)	13	6	7	1
Labour (non-agricultural)	21	10	12	3
Others (pensions, investment, rent etc.)	9	9	10	5
All-India	100	100	100	100

Source: ICE 360 survey, 2021

Way to read this table: Row 2 shows that 20% of Indian households have agriculture as their main source of income, and these 20 per cent of Indian households have a 19 per cent share of India's household income, 18 per cent share of expenditure and 25 per cent share of India's household income surplus.

It must honestly be stated that occupation, despite being such an important characteristic of a consumption-driven economy and India's consumption story, has very little granular data that exists in overly broad categories. One of the big tasks going forward for the Market Research Society of India is to prepare a comprehensive set of occupation codes for future surveys. We know from NSS data that Consumer India is mostly dependent either on agriculture (farms and allied), micro and small businesses, casual labour or informal services work. Are Amazon and Swiggy delivery boys, the urban self-employed workers, the evolution of casual labour with more education? Businesses and marketers (and policymakers) need to note the following:

- Just 10 per cent of households have CWEs that are formally employed. They are punching almost double their weight, with 20 per cent of household income and over 30 per cent of surplus income. However, targeting just them means leaving out the bulk of Consumer India!
- As much as 35 per cent of Indian households are dependent on casual labour as their main source of income.
- As much as 33 per cent of households are dependent on agriculture, despite it contributing a lot less to the economy.

Occupation, jobs and the nature of jobs make up the Achilles' heel of India and the shaky foundation on which its shining unique consumption story rests.

Actually, the issue is less about the quantum of consumption and more about the stability of income and the continued growth of the economy (and hence household income). At the end of this section is a discussion on what the size of India's genuine middle class would be if stability and resilience were added as essential criteria to be given the 'middle class' label; also discussed are the connections between informality and having a stable and growing middle class.

Earlier in this chapter, the poor occupation profile of even the richest 40 per cent of households was discussed. Table 20 below shows the same data on occupation structure for all income groups.

Table 20: Occupation by income group

% of each income group having each occupation

Occupation	Income group				
	Richest 20% Q5	Next 20% Q4	Middle 20% Q3	Next 20% Q2	Poorest 20% Q1
Self-employed in agriculture	17	23	29	19	14
Regular salary—public	17	7	5	4	3
Regular salary—private	33	22	11	7	4
Non-agriculture self-employed	17	16	12	9	8
Casual wage labour					
Agriculture	1	5	16	18	25
Non-agriculture	2	15	21	24	31
Others	10	9	6	8	14
Total	100	100	100	100	100

Source: ICE 360 data

Only the richest 10 per cent of Indian households have a decent occupation profile—12 per cent agriculturist, 58 per cent salaried (36 per cent of which is private), chances being that all of this is formal employment, 14 per cent non-agricultural business and 12 per cent who have retained earnings and investment income.

Education Structure of Consumer India

The tables below give the (weak) education profile of Consumer India and show how much consumption is accounted for by households with varying degrees of education amongst their members or their CWE.

Table 21: College education

Sources	% of households with at least one graduate
Census 2001	12.2
Census 2011	16.7
ICE 360 2021	21.0

As the table shows, having a far better-educated population is still quite some distance away from us. In the absence of widespread vocational education after school finals, the metric of a graduate degree becomes an important dimension of education, though its delivered quality is poor.

The disappointing education profile of even the richest 20 per cent and the next richest 20 per cent have been discussed earlier in this chapter. To complete the picture of the education structure of Consumer India, Table 22 shows the education level of the CWE of the household, i.e., the education level that the household's consumption is 'dependent' on.

Table 22: CWE education by income level of household

% of households with each education level in each income group

CWE Education	Up to Std 4	Std 5–9	School final	Graduate / tech diploma	Post-graduate and above	Total
All-India	27	29	31	10	2	100
Richest 10%	10	17	33	33	7	100
Richest 20%	13	21	37	24	6	100
Next richest 20%	22	32	36	9	2	100
Middle 20%	28	36	31	5	1	100
Next 20%	34	30	30	6	1	100
Poorest 20%	41	27	24	7	1	100

Source ICE 360 data

Even in the richest 10 per cent of households, which we have seen are discontinuously high earners, one-third only have graduate or above degrees, another third have stopped studying after school finals and a quarter have very little schooling. The illiterate numbers in the lowest quintile are hard to believe, so I have combined them with those who have had very little schooling (up to standard 4). The highest education achieved in the household has somewhat better figures, but the quantum of education, let alone its quality, is not transforming rapidly from generation to generation, except in India 2, which benefits from its connect with India 1 (Refer to p. 13).

Table 23 shows the relationship between education and the quantum of consumption.

Table 23: Share of consumption by education level household

Highest education level in the household	% share of all Indian households		
	Share of households	Share of income	Share of surplus income
Up to Primary	31	20	12
School final	46	48	47
Graduate and above	21	31	41

Source: ICE 360 data

While graduates do punch above their population weight in terms of the share of income they have relative to their share of the population, given their smaller number, 70 per cent of Indian household income and about the same on expenditure, and 60 per cent of surplus income still rests with households with lower education levels.

Digital literacy compensates for poor education

While Consumer India is clearly poorly educated, digital literacy is extremely high. It is affordability, not education, that stops people from accessing the goodies that digital has to offer. India has the world's largest number of internet users, who spend more time than most people in the world on the internet. It leads the world in retail digital payment transactions, and 46 per cent of digital real-time transactions in the world are done in India as of 2022.

A survey done for NPCI in May–July 2020 covering low-income, middle-income and high-income states and various income groups within each found that the education level of the person managing digital payments in households engaging in digital payments was not high at all. As much as 42 per cent were qualified below school finals or secondary school certificate (SSC), 39 per cent had finished school and only 20 per cent had a college education.

Watching the barely educated (with only a few years of schooling, mostly primary) learn how to access digital goodies and use smartphones is a continuous reminder of learnability versus formal education, which marketers in India should never ignore.

However, the human capital demographics are depressing, in marked contrast with the consumption statistics.

The Quest for a Meaningful Socio-economic Classification System

In the 1980s, the Market Research Society of India (MRSI) worked on a new socio-economic classification (SEC) for urban

India. The task was to find variables that would closely correlate with income and that could be elicited easily in a doorstep interview.

The variables that emerged were the occupation and education of the CWE. At that time, the need to segment rural India was not felt because it was mostly a homogenous mass of people with very modest incomes, who lived metaphorically in the dark ages, cut off and very different from their urban counterparts—the villagers.

At that time, the finding that occupation and education determined income was very valid because there were a few haves and many have-nots. The rich were minuscule—a constant refrain when I was growing up was, 'Who do you think you are [asking for this]? A Tata or a Birla?' There were no other stereotypes of the moneyed. The middle class comprised people who worked in government and public sector institutions (including the armed forces, railways, public sector banks etc.) and the richer class above them were the few corporate executives who arrived with their perks. The government folks often ruefully described themselves as 'gentlemen of rank with nothing in the bank'. But because of their education and occupation, they were on top of the flattish income and consumption pyramid of a socialist country and were able to educate their children well. A minuscule few went abroad, and the rest studied in the new institutions of excellence in the missionary-led primary school system and the handful of institutions of excellence in higher education—this was India's middle-class children. Today many of the iconic global tech companies and other great global companies, deans of Ivy League schools in America and, last but not least, the World Bank president, are from that swathe of India's middle class. In fact, it is often said that India's best export has been middle-class young people with a good education.

However, in the two decades after liberalization, it became clear that occupation and education were not necessary conditions to earn well. Certain kinds of better education (especially professional degrees) did of course earn better occupations and incomes, but small businessmen or low-skilled but critical workers would earn more than a junior executive—a favourite example in those days was a crane operator in a remote construction site in rural India. And joint families with every member working or running small businesses (three sons, their wives and the parents adding up to eight earning members, working as gym instructors, doing home ironing of clothes, driving an autorickshaw, working in a factory as a packer and in a small beauty parlour as an assistant) and living a lower-middle-class lifestyle also earned as much as someone with more education or a better occupation. And so India's new so-called middle class was born.

With the rise in consumption in rural India, an SEC system for rural India was also required. Developed around 1998, the variables that correlated with income spoke for themselves—the education of the CWE and whether the housing was *kuccha* or *pucca*.[10] The highest income levels of rural India were generally around the same levels as the middle of urban India.

By 2011, the need for a singular system across urban and rural India started to be felt, as the blurring of rural–urban began, and the rural economy started to grow faster, diversifying out of agriculture, while large farms started to get more market-connected.

In their quest for better SEC systems, the MRSI created a new system in 2011—the NCCS, where human development variables of occupation and education have been replaced by the education of the CWE and ownership of eleven durables (ceiling fans, LPG stove, colour TV, two-wheeler, refrigerator, washing machine, laptop, four-wheeler car/van/jeep, air conditioner, electricity and agricultural land) and have created twelve classifications based on the number of durables owned and the education of the CWE and assets owned. This is the NCCS that has been discussed earlier in the chapter. This list of durables was intended to allow surveyors to discriminate both at the higher end of the income spectrum and the lower end.

It is time to review this again, as the prices of durables have dropped, incomes have risen and loans for durables are very easy to get—ownership of durables is not indicating income differences as strongly as it used to. Also, electricity is now in every village, and well-off non-agricultural households may not be landowners at all.

The MRSI then looked at an alternative system based purely on social parameters—CWE occupation and education of the highest educated male adult and highest educated female adult. These results are shown on the left of Chart 4.

The grid on the left shows the twelve affluence classes based on the present system of ownership of consumer durables and occupation of the CWE. The grid on the right shows the twelve classes based on human development variables of the proposed new system under discussion, the occupation of the CWE and the highest education attained in the household by the highest educated male and the female member.

Chart 4: Comparison of NCCS (durables and CWE education) and ISEC (occupation of CWE and education of highest educated male and female)

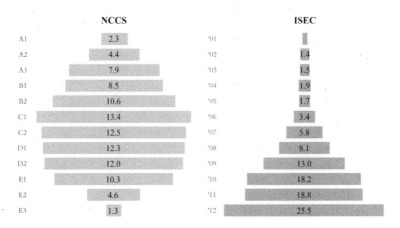

Source: IRS 2017, courtesy Media Research Users Council MRUC
The chart on the left is a classification of consumption potential or affluence based on ownership of durables i.e., consumption already happening; the chart on the right is based purely on human development variables

Clearly, Consumer India is still very sadly triangular-shaped on social parameters, with a fat bottom and a very narrow top. Ownership of durables, however, as an indicator of affluence, has moved to a pyramid shape with a fat middle. This essentially reinforces the point that social indicators and consumption are not very strongly correlated, except for certain categories of consumption, whose cultural label still attracts 'not for people like us' interpretations, perhaps because of how they are communicated.

Urban India is, however, showing some upward movement towards becoming a diamond from a pyramid, with a broader top, while rural India is still stuck at a pyramid stage.

Chart 5: ISEC grades for Urban versus Rural

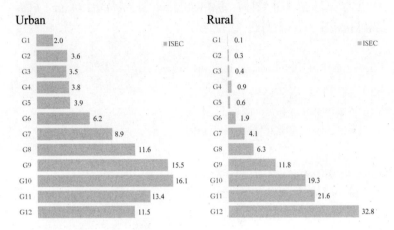

Source: IRS 2017 Survey, new ISEC classification system; G1 highest G12 lowest

Section V: How to Think about India's Middle Class

The question that arises then, is this: why worry about poor demographics of occupation or education in the context of consumption?

The answer lies in the stability of consumption that a genuine middle class can bring, with stable income and resilient consumption and the ability to grow the quality of consumption as well and thus attract investments in a big way. This section is based on work done jointly with Dr Yuwa Hedrick-Wong.[11]

India's Middle-Class Consumption: How Stable and How Resilient?

A favourite pastime of India's business analysts and media over the years has been to estimate the size of India's middle class, a critical indicator of the current and future health of India's household consumption, hence India's economy. Estimates of India's middle class are as many as the number of people engaged in this quest. Perhaps this is because of a lack of clarity on what characteristics the middle class must have in order to qualify for the label, despite all the literature on the subject from scholars around the world. The result is several groupings of heterogeneous households, all labelled 'middle class' based on benchmarks of other countries, subjective judgements with very wide income ranges, yardsticks of consumption of consumer durables and amenities or a magic threshold of income at which consumption is supposed to 'take off', based on developed world cost structures (ask Jio and HUL if they believe this).

In reality, India's genuine middle class is less than half of the 400–500 million number that floats around. Seeing the large economic impact such a small genuine middle class has achieved, instead of calling victory, it is time to obsess over how to significantly expand it to help India turbocharge the economy to achieve its fullest potential.

What characteristics should a genuine middle class have and why? And basis that, what is the best estimate of the size of India's genuine middle class?

The economic concept of 'middle class', on which abundant literature exists, is that a genuine middle class should provide a certain quantum of consumption that is stable and resilient because of how the income to consume is generated (the nature of occupation); further, it should have enough surpluses after routine expenditure to help the middle class weather economic downturns and be able to bounce back without having to contract its consumption too much for too long. This is where many of the so-called middle-class households in India do not qualify.

Such stable and resilient demand will give investors the confidence to invest which, in turn, creates a virtuous cycle of creating jobs and further strengthen the middle class. Surplus income that is reasonable, stable and resilient also contributes to the savings health of the economy.

For a middle class to be a long-term, high-commitment investment thesis for businesses, in addition to the stability and resilience of its consumption, there needs to be a strong foundation that enables continuous improvement in income levels. This will lead to more and better-quality consumption as well. A genuine middle-class household is one where consumption behaviour steadily shifts upwards from price sensitivity to benefit sensitivity. This, in turn, stimulates another virtuous cycle of powerful, diverse and better-quality supply responses.

The charts below show that when these criteria are applied, India's genuine middle class is much smaller than most popular estimates. It sits in the richest 10–20 per cent of Indian households and not in the middle of the income spectrum. D10 and D9, the richest top two deciles of households, qualify on income criteria. However, their occupation profile is worrisome. Only 60 per cent of D10 and less than half of D9 have regular salaries. In D9, a large portion of them are privately employed and, given the known fact of minuscule formal employment, are most likely to be informally employed. Income dependence on small agricultural land and informal non-agricultural occupations is 42 per cent for D9 and about a quarter of D10, making them inherently unstable. Education demographics of CWEs are not conducive to upward mobility into value-added, high-skilled jobs—just 20 per cent of D9 and 40 per cent of D10 have college degrees or technical diplomas. Realistically, this reduces the size of the genuine, fully-formed middle class even further to 40–50 million households. This is still larger than the population of many developed countries. However, it is far below India's own potential.

India is still quite some way off from having a genuine middle class that can power its economy. Middle India, the middle 60 per cent of households in the middle of the income spectrum, should have been the genuine middle class of India and has been neglected. India's future lies in building a genuine middle-class several times larger than it is now. Imagine the impact on the economy if that number was three times what it is now.

Table 24A: Where is the middle class on income-based criteria

Income-based criteria	Deciles or 10% slabs of households based on annual household income (D10 richest									
	D10 (richest)	D9	D8	D7	D6	D5	D4	D3	D2	D1 (low)
World Bank global income group definitions	Rich	Upper middle	Upper middle	Middle	Middle	Low	Low	Low	Low	Low
Surplus income to total income ratio 2021 (%)	39	27	13	14	4	Negative	Negative	Negative	Negative	Negative
Change in absolute surplus income: 2021 versus 2016 (pre economic slowdown and pandemic)	+6		-50		-98		Collapsed		Collapsed	
Resilience: % decline in surplus income to total income ratio: 2021 vs 2016	-29		-56		Collapsed		Collapsed		Collapsed	Collapsed
Contribution to all India's household surplus income 2021 (%)	68	24	8	6	2	Negative	Negative	Negative	Negative	Negative

■ Qualifies as middle class   ■ Does not qualify

D10 to D1 are 10 per cent-sized slabs of households based on income, starting from the richest 10 per cent of households, decile D10, to the poorest 10 per cent, decile D1. Dark areas indicate deciles that qualify as a genuine middle class, while the light ones indicate those that do not. The only two deciles that qualify are D10 and D9. We have considered even the richest 10 per cent as middle class because, based on durable ownership, the label of rich applies to a very, very small sliver (according to the NCCS classification system of affluence based on durables ownership, in the top 2.5 per cent of households, there is 70–80 per cent ownership of air conditioners and cars; that drops to 30–32 per cent in the next 2.5 per cent).

Table 24B: Where is the genuine middle class in terms of stable occupations to move to value-added jobs?

Occupation on which household depends (% of households in each)	Deciles or 10% slabs of households based on annual household income (D10 richest)			
	D10	D9	D8	D7
Regular salaried job—private	36	30	23	21
Regular salaried job—public	22	13	8	7
Total regular salaried households (sum of two columns above)	**58**	**43**	**31**	**28**
Agricultural self-employment	12	22	23	24
Non-agricultural self-employment	14	20	18	15
Others (retired, pensioner, remittances, etc.)	12	13	9	11
Casual labour—non-agricultural	1	3	11	18
Casual labour—agricultural	1	1	4	5
Total casual labour	**2**	**4**	**15**	**23**
Total	100	100	100	100

Table 24C: Where is the genuine middle class in terms of education to move to value-added jobs?

Education of CWE (ability for upward mobility)	Deciles or 10% slabs of households based on annual household income (D10 richest)			
	D10	D9	D8	D7
No formal schooling	9	12	18	18
Up to Std 9	19	28	33	37
Finished matriculation/higher secondary	33	40	37	35
Technical diploma	13	5	2	1
Graduate	20	10	8	7
Post-graduate	5	4	1	1
Professional higher education/doctorate	2	1	<1	<1
Total	100	100	100	100

■ Qualifies as middle class   ■ Does not qualify

India's Consumption Future Lies in Building a Genuine Middle-class

To realize the country's economic ambition, a large, expanding and increasingly prosperous genuine middle class is needed—one that has income stability, resilience and the ability to upgrade to grow its income steadily through value-added work. Why is the middle class so stunted in India? We believe that it is both a cause and consequence of the widespread informal sector, which is commonly estimated to account for 90 per cent of employment, generating only one-third of the value added in the economy. It is huge, with limited efficiency because of its many constraints and is a low-productivity trap that chokes off the formation of a genuine middle class.

Typically, informal workers either work as individual casual labour or in micro-enterprises with very small operations, having less than ten employees under conditions of instability in both employment and income. Conditions in the informal sector vitiate workers' efforts to get ahead and become middle class regardless of the legendary Indian hard work, capability and highly entrepreneurial spirit. As a result, Indians are trapped in situations where they are unable to increase their productivity and income by working with better tools, easily learning new skills, getting the effort-multiplier benefit of teamwork and accessing the full suite of reasonably priced and regulated financial services. The nature of temporary or contract workers in the informal economy disincentivizes the employer from investing in productivity-enhancing tools and training workers to use them, since the pay-off time horizon is longer than the workers' tenure; besides, informal employers themselves do not have the wherewithal to invest in worker productivity.

The informal sector also denies workers the opportunity to benefit from teamwork. A key feature of the new world, as we all know, is the need for workers to collaborate with others with complementary skills, such that they can collectively perform and benefit from complex and high value-added tasks that none of them could do on their own. However, in the informal sector, because of the transient nature of the workforce, even if a person is part of a work crew of thousands (an example is delivery services or large construction projects), working with others as a stable team does not happen. There is a large contingent of what we call solo service providers even among higher-skilled occupations such as carpenters, tailors and auto mechanics. And even when they are a part of digital aggregator platforms, they are still largely on their own. The ILO has estimated that in 2017 a full one-third of Indian workers in the informal sector are the so-called 'own account workers'. The result is persistently low productivity.

The problems of access to financing for informal workers and micro-enterprises that are not a part of any formal supply chain are well-known, and we will not reiterate them. The ratio of domestic credit to GDP, which measures how much credit has been extended to people and businesses benchmarked against the size of the economy, is far lower in India than in, say, China or the USA. It has also been stagnant in India for the entire decade ending in 2022, while it expanded in all the key economies in the world.

For all these reasons, the informal sector in India undermines the economy's ability to create a large, genuine middle class. India's stunted middle class is also the flip side of its stunted manufacturing sector, a significant proportion of which is fragmented and carried out mostly by small and micro enterprises, which do not possess the competitive efficiency to grow and create formal jobs. Large competitive manufacturing exists mostly in the small formal sector accounting for a minor fraction of the labour force.

Historically, manufacturing is the well-trodden path to economic development. The Harvard economist Dani Rodrik has characterized manufacturing as the elevator that lifts a country's productivity rapidly from the basement to the penthouse. Make in India is the crucial conduit through which formal jobs and a genuine middle class could rapidly expand despite a modestly educated workforce, which is India's other reality. The post-World War II manufacturing sector in the US enabled someone with a high school education or less to earn a middle-class income. Manufacturing in India so far has not been able to do this.

Given the success of India's IT sector, could India leapfrog to IT services to fuel the expansion of the middle class, bypassing manufacturing? The National Association of Software and Service Companies (NASSCOM) data shows that even using the broader definition of the sector, which includes low-end functions such as call centres, the total employment is 4.5 million, which is still a drop in the ocean of India's large labour force. Can the rest of the services sector create jobs that have all the ingredients we discussed so far as to qualify as being truly formal and hence deliver productivity-driven income boosts and fuel high-quality entrepreneurship? So far, we have not seen it happen on a large scale. Even platform aggregators are unlikely to deliver it by the very nature of their business model, though they do address some of the limitations of 'own account workers' such as market access, improved pricing power and better buyer power of ingredients needed for business such as finance or consumables supplies.

The Indian economy is at a fork in the road: it can either choose a policy push that delivers a large, vibrant and prosperous middle class or a business-as-usual growth story with a massive informal sector that increased consumption but not of the calibre of a genuine middle class. In order to rapidly expand India's genuine middle class with all its manifold benefits, there appears to be no shortcut to creating a large-scale manufacturing sector that can drive formal employment. This, coming on top of the modern welfare state that has been built in the past decade, will truly transform India's consumption and economic trajectory on many fronts.

What Was the Purpose of This Chapter?

It was to show the structure of Consumer India. How much is the income? Where and how is it distributed? How well-educated is India's consumer base? How does it earn the income that drives its famed consumption?

This will help businesses to understand the opportunity more fully, warts and all, pain and gain. It is a large consumer base of modestly educated people but digitally smart, a huge mass market straddling urban and rural India, the vast geographic spread even of the rich, the occupation and education demographics even of the rich and the consumption levels apparently quite divorced from human development levels. Is there a mega opportunity there? It is a large market of a lot of people with modest incomes, earning a little bit each, which adds up to a lot. However, relative to the rest of the developed world, even the richest 10 per cent of Indian households are poor—in fact, just around the poverty line of America.

Appendix: Income Measurement Practices in India

As with a lot of things in India, so too with income data, it is the Tower of Babel out there and there are many versions of household income data and many sizes and definitions of middle classes in business presentations, media articles and investor pitches. It varies depending on who is putting it out, which part of the income pyramid they are interested in and how they got their numbers (many, including glitzy global consulting company reports, don't say). Official income statistics are hard to come by in India because government data is around household expenditure and not income. Income tax data is not very helpful, because only 8.1 million people pay income tax in India today. Even assuming one person per household (likely to be more), that leaves a data blank for 300 million households. Given the heterogeneity of Indian households on so many dimensions, doing surveys that are representative of all Indian households and with large enough samples to provide meaningful levels of disaggregation and stratification is expensive, elaborate and time-consuming. On top of that, income measurement is tricky and cannot be done in a short doorstep interview; what constitutes income in a country with so many occupations and so much informal employment needs to be thought through and is difficult to survey using simple measures. The willingness of respondents to share information is not such a big issue in India, though under-reporting of income at the higher end does tend to happen.

Given these challenges, there are very few organizations whose methodology and sampling have the required level of rigour and whose income data is sufficiently reliable. One of them whose data I use is called the ICE 360 dataset and has been done in 2014, 2016 and 2021, modelled after the NCAER surveys of 1995 and 2004 so that the data is comparable over time. In addition, the Market Research Society of India (MRSI) and the Media Research Users Council are two industry bodies that conduct the industry-accepted socio-economic classification of Indian households using surrogate variables for income (affluence) such as ownership of durables and occupation of CWEs. There are lots of income distributions of Indian households that figure in the glitzy reports of the Indian offices of global consulting companies, and these get used and quoted widely (yet another example of the power of the brand); however, they rarely provide the source of the data. While some say that their proprietary surveys are the basis of their income estimation, they are silent or hazy on survey details, such as sample universe, sample size, data collection locations and other key details. This Appendix provides a detailed discussion on details of the methodology and sampling.

It could be that the income survey was an add-on single question asked as a by-product of some other survey specific to a product category or something else that makes the income data from the survey not truly representative of all Indian households and/or not collected rigorously enough in terms of the questioning methodology.

As an illustration, here is a comparison of two recent reports containing income distribution data, one for the ICE 360 survey and one from a large global consulting firm. The ICE 360 survey said it covered 23 states and union territories and created a sampling frame of 2,00,000 households, where basic data on household population was collected (methodology of listing households for the frame clear), from which 40,000 households were selected using probability sampling. The reference period for response is FY 2021. The second report said that their income estimation was based on a sample of '*more than 8,200 consumers*' surveyed in 2019, and a 'fresh survey of 1,200 in 2020' to understand COVID impact. On location, they said the biggest city surveyed was XXX and the smallest was YYY (incidentally, both were in north India). They made no mention of how many were in between or how they were selected or how data from them was extrapolated to the universe. Income estimation adopted by ICE 360 is entirely based on income measured by the survey, while the other report talked of using these proprietary surveys alongside methods that 'include regressing household income against economic growth'. The assumption is that 'cities move up two steps over a decade', so presumably, ten-year-old metro data is used as a surrogate for any tier-2 town income distribution ten years later. Also, it included 'mapping against countries which were the same level of economic development as India a decade ago'.

I put my money and my judgement on the ICE 360 survey without being partisan, despite my association with the surveys when they were done. It has fewer assumptions and far greater transparency on the survey methodology and how the survey data was used to come up with income distributions.

In summary, the income measurement methodology used and survey details of the ICE 360 survey are based on the measurement methodology of household income prescribed by the Canberra Group,[12] and the actual income for the reference year 2020–21 has been measured for a set of survey households that are representative of all Indian households. Household income of Indian households has been estimated based on this data. As is usual in surveys of any kind, the estimated national income from the survey falls short of the official number for household income that is derived from national accounts and put out by the government of India. Even the government's official household expenditure survey, the NSS, captures only about half of the total expenditure (PFCE—private final consumption expenditure) given in National Accounts. The ICE 360 survey does a bit better in its capture of household income.

The method followed by me is to use the survey data to determine the distribution of income i.e., what share of the total estimated income different income groups have (groupings of households according to their income), and then apply that share to the government-given number of personal disposable income (PDI) for Indian households (PDI is household income net of taxes). So if households are grouped into three income groups and the total share of household income in each class, as measured by the survey, is 50 per cent, 30 per cent and 10 per cent respectively, and the total PDI as per national accounts (government statistics) is Rs 1000, then the total pooled income of all households in each income group will be 50/30/10 per cent of Rs 1000 or Rs 400, 300 and 100, respectively. Dividing the pooled income in each income group by the number of households in that group gives the average per household income for households in each income group or income class (the two words used interchangeably). Of course, this has the assumption that the income measured in all income groups is equally inaccurate, but it is a 'can live with' assumption that still makes the household income numbers usable. Since many people around the world use GDP per capita as a surrogate for income, this household income distribution obtained from the survey can be applied to net national income or GDP instead of

PDI, as the user preference may be. However, PDI would be more appropriate, since the survey measures personal household income, and very few people pay income tax.

Table 25 gives more detailed data on equivalence of Indian household income with World Bank global definitions.

Table 25: Income deciles and World Bank global income class equivalence (2021–22 nominal income-based)

World Bank global classification	Income deciles from ICE 360 Survey and PDI									
	D10 Highest	D9	D8	D7	D6	D5	D4	D3	D2	D1 Lowest
High income	■									
Upper middle 3 (highest)										
Upper middle 2 (middle)		■								
Upper middle 1 (lowest)			■							
Middle 3 (highest)										
Middle 2 (middle)				■						
Middle 1 (lowest)					■					
Lower 3 (highest)						■				
Lower 2 (middle)							■	■		
Lower 1 (lowest)									■	■

THE FUTURE OF INDIA'S CONSUMPTION

 Consumer India Structure Story

 Consumer Behaviour Story

 Supply Side Story

4

Understanding Consumer India's Behaviour

A lot has been written about this in media stories and books, and 'the changing Indian consumer' is a favourite conference topic. However, given the structure story of the many Indias, all these anecdotes and observations of how different parts of the elephant behave need to be distilled into a holistic view of the nature of the beast.

This chapter looks at key shapers of behaviour—aspiration, dignity, Indian identity, brand orientation, the phenomenon of monster consumers, how to understand and navigate heterogeneity of the market for strategy development, and how to read change in the confusing way in which Consumer India changes.

Shapers of Consumer India's Consumption Behaviour

A macro-consumer view of the people of India

Consumer India, as the previous chapter on structure has demonstrated, is a fragmented and complex hydra-headed monster, based on just its economy, demographics and living conditions. Add to that a layer of different social and cultural factors affecting different parts of Consumer India (including community, region, politics and language), and different levels of exposure to different worlds outside, and it gets even more complex.

Requests asking me to speak on the topic of 'Indian Consumer Behaviour' or 'Changing Consumer Behaviour in India' terrify me. How does one capture the enormity of behaviour variations in Consumer India? No matter what one could say, the opposite would also be true in some audience members' recent experience! Therefore, for reasons of both prudence and competence, this chapter will not attempt the near-impossible task of chronicling different kinds of consumer behaviour and different patterns of consumption.

The focus of this chapter will instead be on understanding the lives, mind spaces and attitudes that shape the behaviour of the people who comprise Consumer India. This is useful because consumption and brands do not live in the narrow confines of a market space but exist as a part of the larger canvas of people's lives. Serving a consumer base without understanding what makes it tick does not make for winning businesses, sound market strategies or creating brands that deeply resonate with consumers.

This chapter has three sections:

1. Shapers of Consumer India's consumption behaviour: A few important themes that are common and relevant to all income groups.
2. Structure and drivers of heterogeneity in Consumer India and how to think about consumer segmentation.
3. How India changes and reading change in Consumer India

As everywhere in this book, this chapter will also examine many of the commonly held hypotheses and theories about Consumer India to test their validity and change, nuance or caveat them as the case may require.

Section I: Shapers of Consumer India's Consumption Behaviour

This section identifies and explores a few important themes that are common across all of Consumer India and shape the consumption behaviour of all income groups.

A Tectonic Shift from Acceptance to Aspiration, Facilitated by Credit

Aspirational India is a tectonic shift from the pre-liberalization days when we would often hear consumers of lower-income groups tell us in focus groups, 'This is not for me, this is for the *badey log* (big people).' Now, there is a strong statement of, 'I want to have something like that, be it products or experiences.' A car is obviously not affordable, but a bike and a taxi for special family outings is. Now, having what celebrities have has become easy with social media. Copies of actress Alia Bhatt's mehendi pattern and cheap knock-offs of her wedding dress are available. Influencers and beauticians of every social class tell you how to use make-up like celebrities do and style yourself at a price point that you can afford. As ad man Santosh Desai puts it, the big shift is that 'life is not a condition to be endured but a product to be experienced'. Aspiration-led living is the opposite of the way it used to be. The attitude and mindset shift is from 'this is what I have and how do I manage best within it' to 'this is what I want, so how do I manage to get it'. We see this resulting in choices which can best be described as 'stretch for more, do not settle for less'. Borrow and buy the higher category car or two-wheeler or buy a second-hand one rather than settle for the easily affordable small car, even if it means waiting a bit, buying a pre-owned vehicle or taking a loan.

Credit or borrowing for consumption once considered a very dangerous thing, is now acceptable and 'normal' to Consumer India. Amazon and consumer durables stores and travel sites helpfully ask you, at the time of checking out, if you want to pay by EMI, that is, equated monthly instalments of credit. Credit is also morally purified. Its cultural label has changed from indebtedness, which can lead to ruin, to being the working capital for life and the helping hand that everybody needs to reach their goals. Financial services companies have been exploiting this attitude shift leading to the regulators and the courts coming down hard and framing laws to curb irresponsible lending that leads to imprudent borrowing, and strong-arm tactics for recovery that lead to customer stress and even suicides. An example of this is what happened to the microfinance industry in 2010 leading to a new law in 2011 that banned MFIs from approaching the doorstep of their customers, lengthened the loan collection cycles and told lenders that they had to get government approval to give a second loan to the same lender. The Reserve Bank of India, India's banking regulator has issued a charter of customer rights for banks and non-banking financial services companies (NBFC) that includes the 'right to suitability', where 'only products and services that are appropriate to the understanding and financial conditions of the customers may be offered to them.' It is a caveat venditor (let the seller beware) as far as enforcing this right is concerned.

Consumer India now does a lot of goal-based planning— decide the goal and how to fund it. Households that manage money well prosper, while those that don't end up with credit card debts and the embarrassment of assets being repossessed.

Thus far, Indians have been prudent, even more so modest income Indians. Today, compared to the rest of the world, Indian households are much lower on household debt to GDP ratios. In 2022, this ratio was between 65 and 85 per cent for countries in the developed world including China and Japan, while India stood at between 35 and 36 per cent in 2022.

State Bank of India research states that the bulk (86 per cent) of the increase in household indebtedness between financial year (FY) 2021 and 2023 went into home loans and creating other physical assets. 55 per cent of the increase in retail credit was to fund housing, education and vehicles. The report is clear that the decrease in household savings between FY21 and FY23 has been offset by the increase in physical assets of households.[1]

However, when there is a generational transition and those born after 2000 become the ruling age cohort of householders, Consumer India's relationship with debt and their ability to manage their indebtedness well is an area of future concern in a 'watch this space carefully' sense. This cohort has seen credit go from a seller's market to a buyer's market, especially with the advent of fintech and its offers of instant credit. They have shed the horror of 'what will the neighbours say if the debt collector shows up at my door'. Easy availability of credit has made them more transactional and 'equal' with their lender than in the past decades when getting a loan was very difficult. A vehicle lender in the rural areas described how the new generation of borrowers says, 'Come and re-possess the vehicle, I cannot pay EMI for some time now, and I will get another loan and buy another vehicle later.' This, of course, leaves the lender with the price risk on the repossessed vehicle! The good news is that credit bureaus now make it hard for people to take multiple loans if they have defaulted on even one of them.

Aspiration, goal-based planning, and the new credit culture (both from the supply side and the consumer side) augur very well for consumption. Informational resources also fuel aspiration. Consumer India's problem lies not in its lack of aspiration but in its ability to earn more to be able to afford better and to have what it takes to be able to earn more. Fortunately, Consumer India's optimism that the future will be better even if today is tough is usually very high, perhaps because it has, by and large, been so for them.

As the next part of the book—which is about the supply side—will discuss, consumers are deeply desirous of many things, but they struggle to balance the aspiration–income gap. Are suppliers ready to innovate affordable, acceptable supply to tap into this groundswell of aspiration?

Understanding the Contours of 'Aspiration'

If I had a rupee for every time the word 'aspiration' has been used in the last decade to qualify Indian people or consumption or target group definitions or voter choices, I would be very rich indeed. This section tries to put some flesh around the idea of the 'aspirational Indian consumer'.

High aspiration meets hard reality: Consumption is a big balancing act

Consumer India's consumption is located at the crossroads of high aspiration for a better life, woefully inadequate quality and quantity of public goods and amenities and modest incomes which, as we discussed in the occupation section, are also unstable. Even as incomes increase and public goods improve, so does aspiration increase (because there is a long way to go for most Indians to have even the basics of a good life, and because information resources are available to them so that they can imagine that better life more concretely).

This gap between where they want to be, what they want to have and what the hard reality of income and availability of quality public goods makes their lives—and their consumption behaviour—one big balancing act. Marketers who fail to understand this often do not see the severe inter-category consumption that exists and are bewildered by the sudden changes in consumer behaviour with respect to their category, when nothing much appears to have happened to cause it.

Aspiration for a better quality of life is universal and multifaceted

Every socio-economic class of India is steeped in aspiration. The rich and the poor alike aspire to climb the next rung of the ladder of a good life—a better house, better transport, better education for the children, better healthcare, better entertainment, better experiences and indulgences.

Take housing for example. At the bottom-most rung, the aspiration is to do better than a mud hut and get a pucca house, while at the top it is to move to an even bigger, better-located, more luxurious house and have a second home in the hills or near the sea. And there are several shades of this in the middle.

In the case of education, at the lower incomes, it is to get your child to an *Anganwadi* (centres in rural India set up and run by the government, that provide non-formal education and nutrition supplements for pre-school children, among other basic healthcare services) and then into a government school; at the next level, it is to get your child away from the government school system into a private school (a lot of data exists on how even the lower-income groups are moving away from the poorly functioning government school system into 'mom-and-pop' private schools because the child needs to learn English and computers and have teachers who show up every day). At higher income groups, parents aspire to send their children to good Indian colleges often paying capitation fees (donations to the college corpus); or, given how hard it is to get into decent colleges in India, they aspire to send their children abroad at very steep fees. Parents who have had the best education in India aspire for their children to have the Ivy League education that they could not.

Even the most modest-income families will send their children to some kind of extra tuition because the parents themselves are not educated enough to monitor the child's studies. Higher-income people will send their children to more expensive coaching in order to make them score much more or crack competitive exams. At the top, there are very high-priced education consultants (in the range of Rs 10–20 lakh) who help children from very high-income groups build their resumes and get into the best colleges around the world.

At the lower income groups, the aspiration is to be able to access a private hospital, where they feel the care (not the capability—that is still seen to reside in government hospitals, where they go as a last resort) is better and hence chances of getting cured are greater. At the highest levels of income, it is the big brand name hospitals in America that they aspire to go to because the capabilities are far greater than the ones in India.

Modest-income families aspire to have conveniences that save labour and improve productivity (refrigerators, washing machines, mixer grinders) and basic comforts (furniture, air conditioners, room heaters in places with extreme weather), better transportation and travel conditions to enable them to widen their footprint of activity with some degree of comfort, convenience and affordability. This will provide them access to things and places that are further away, including well-paying jobs, cheaper housing, schools and hospitals in bigger towns; less time and effort in all the logistics of living; last but not least, enjoyable experiences and affordable indulgences for the entire family. There is a whole Maslow's hierarchy embedded in just the physiological and safety improvements that Indians want in their lives.

Large categories of 'aspirational' consumption: Basic things that improve quality of life, not higher-order gratification

Consumer India's spending is, in large part, pragmatic and utilitarian, directed towards things that improve quality of life. A significant part of this is what policy advisor Akhilesh Tilotia refers to in his book *The Making of India* as the private cost of public (goods) failures.

Table 1 shows the spending on quality-of-life basics and shows how the patterns change as incomes increase. The incremental pool of expenditure in every category is so apparent with increases in income, underscoring the argument made *ad infinitum* in this book that aspiration is uniform and the only spoilsport is income levels.

Looking at expenditure by value spaces across product categories, a major category comprises *productivity tools* to enable the release of earning time or rest time to make one fit to earn.

Table 1: Expenditure patterns of households

Item	% of income spent by each income group on each category			
	Poorest 15%	Middle 50%	Next 30%	Richest 4%
Housing and related utilities	6	9	11	10
Healthcare and fitness	7	7	8	8
Education	4	5	8	8
Conveyance, tours and travels	3	4	6	8
Beverages, packaged food, eating out	4	6	9	13
Consumer durables	1	1	2	2
Share of total expenditure on these categories (% of total expenditure)	25	32	44	49
Expenditure index (total quantum of expenditure)	1	6	20	100

Source: ICE360 data, 2020-21

Way to read this table: The last row shows the total amount spent on these categories by each group. The richest 4 per cent is 100, then the next richest 30 per cent spend 20 and so on. The second last row shows what share of total income these categories account for the poorest 25 per cent of households spend 25 per cent of their total expenditure on these categories, the middle 50 per cent spend 32 per cent while the richest 4 per cent spend 49 per cent of their household expenditure on these categories. Moving on to columns, the second column shows that the poorest 15 per cent of households spend 6 per cent of their total expenditure on housing and related categories, another 7 per cent on fitness and so on. The next three columns show the same data for other income groups.

In a mostly self-employed country, if you don't or can't show up at work, you don't earn. Cell phones and two-wheelers are must-have productivity tools. A refrigerator and LPG gas enable the modest-income woman to make and keep food for the family while she works longer hours or to be more efficient in packing the family lunchboxes (and being able to get everyone, including herself, to get to work on time).

Another value space is that of 'cost-effective quality of life improvers'. All categories of *digital-related spends* are included here—for example, buying smartphones so that you can connect with scattered families and migrant husbands and fathers on video calls and save time and travel costs, doing money transfers without paying a go-between and entertaining yourself very cheaply. A survey done by one of my student groups showed that the largest users of cellular data were security guards, who have a boring job and no access to Wi-Fi, unlike office job workers. A lot of data on internet usage behaviour by income groups is available. In India in the 1970s and 1980s, it used to be said that the price of onions would determine the outcome of elections in the country. Today, I would venture to say that it is the price of data. A government that fails to keep data rates low will have a very, very upset mass consumer base for sure.

Once-in-a-while indulgences and experiences, such as a trip to a multiplex, a small restaurant, an amusement park or just Chowpatty Beach for ice cream, as the purse may permit, is another value space of aspirational spending. For upper-income consumers, it almost certainly is travel abroad or in India for new experiences. The experience economy is here too in full force, and the tourism and hospitality industries are yet to catch up with it.

So, aspirational goods in India are, mainly, not about fancy brand labels or higher-order needs. Of course, *status signalling* or *self-expression* is a very important thing, but it is the ability to have access to things and experiences and post them on social media that does the job as well or better than having an expensive 'badge brand' that fewer people will get to see. In the modest income groups, social media and even WhatsApp display pictures can be cheaply changed every week to make a statement (free of cost)—on a borrowed motorcycle with a borrowed jacket and dark glasses or in front of interesting-looking buildings or houses, selfies at interesting locations or selfies with celebrities and so on.

Shift from Benevolence and Dependence to Rights and Dignity of Self-Reliance

India has historically been a society with a high power distance. Power distance, which I have discussed in my previous books, is one of the constructs of Dutch social psychologist Geert Hofstede and refers to the extent to which those without power accept the rights of those with power to have it. More precisely, it is the extent to which power is unequally distributed and the acceptance of it by the less powerful.

However, power distance has been steadily decreasing as legislations bridging power gaps start taking effect. Even though it takes several generations for the changes to become mainstream, the 'rights-based' relationship between weaker sections of society and government has replaced the previous relationship of '*mai baap sarkar*' (mother–father government). In the November 2023 elections in Telangana, the chief minister said at his rally that the opposition party in the state will give you goodies as if they 'carry you on their hip' (a colloquial phrase for 'give you support as if you are helpless and they are your benefactors') but his party would help them prosper. Another minority leader said something to the effect that if a certain party came to power, they would say, 'You do your rituals and leave the rest to us, we will take care of you,' but that what was needed, instead, for his people, was for them to improve their education and earning potential.

The right to work (rural employment guarantee scheme, NREGA), right to education (RTE), right to information (RTI), right to food, and right to direct benefit transfers (DBTs) are just some examples of the legislation and programmes over time that have driven this change.

The Narendra Modi-led decade of building a modern welfare state has also dispensed with local bureaucracy (middlemen). DBTs and subsidies from the government going directly into individual bank accounts have driven this change very profoundly. Again, at the election rally discussed earlier, the chief minister talked of how benefits to them were coming 'ting-ting-ting into your cell phones' (referring to text notifications from the bank when money is deposited) and they did not have to beg the local government officials for it or pay them a bribe.

Schemes like LPG gas, micro insurance, Ayushman Bharat and Jan Dhan bank accounts have added enormously to the dignity felt by the average Indian. I can feel it in the voice of the *dhobi*, who says to me when I offer him cash, '*Khatey mein dal do*' (send it to my bank account), or the fact that my maid at home and I order LPG gas cylinders at the same time and she gets hers earlier because it is all automated now.

As discussed in my previous book, the legislations passed over the years giving women rights to property, to end marriages citing 'irretrievable breakdowns' and reserved seats in various political and other institutions have also created a significant number of visible women role models and expanded the concept of roles of women.

The most-watched television serial in Hindi is *Anupama*. That the eponymous protagonist walks out of her marriage when her husband brings home another woman, stands on her own feet by opening a dance school, marries a second time and 'lives with dignity' is the big theme of this show. It is a similar case in the Telugu serial *Grihalakshmi*, where the lead decides to divorce a husband who is living with another woman and introduces concepts such as 'I need to grow' and 'I have to fulfil my dreams.' The idea of 'I need to try to stand on my own feet' is very strongly embedded into both these popular programmes.

A New Comfort with Being Indian and a New Indian Identity

Taking cues from how senior political leaders represent India to the world

The body language and words on the global stage of India's prime minister and external affairs minister are a symbol of a new Indian Identity. It is not an identity rooted in being an old civilization or a champion of yesteryear but rooted in today. In a speech to the United Nations Security Council, Prime Minister Narendra Modi pushed for India to have a permanent seat at the UN Security Council by saying, 'How can the UN Security Council claim to speak to the world when its most populous country and its largest democracy is not a permanent member?'[2] Clips of India's no-holds-barred, plain-speaking foreign minister to Western audiences, calling out the West's double standards when it comes to India and their own countries are favourites for circulation on WhatsApp. This is the relationship between India and the world that Young India sees today, not to mention sidelights of 'be yourself', like India's prime minister fasting at a White House dinner in 2014 because of the Navratri festival, reported by the *Wall Street Journal* (25 September 2014) as 'India's Prime Minister Narendra Modi to Fast During White

House Dinner.' The new 'no nonsense' India is often seen in cartoons doing the rounds on WhatsApp. One has the former prime minister holding his head in his hands and saying, 'The possibility of terrorist attacks gives me sleepless nights' and the present prime minister looking the world in the eye and saying, 'We will not tolerate any terror attacks on India.'

English is no longer the Holy Grail

English is still seen to be a 'premium' language—it enables greater salaries and English-medium schools are perceived to be better in terms of quality of education. The educated upper class is known to speak English fluently, so there is definitely a status associated. For all these reasons and more, English knowledge is an aspirational goal. However, for even the well-educated youth of today, the Europe-like relegation of English to the second place below the vernacular is quite usual. It is not as if English has diminished in value, but that vernacular languages have found their place in the arena of status. Even on prestigious college campuses, one hears more vernacular spoken in corridors and cafes than maybe even fifteen years ago. Of the 760 million active Internet users in India, 500 plus are not English-literate users. The prestigious civil services exam is now conducted in English and Hindi, and some of the papers can be taken in vernacular languages too.

On OTT platforms too English is the minority language. According to the FICCI–EY report on the Indian entertainment and media industry, in 2022, over half of the total OTT content viewing was in regional languages. There are at least fifteen popular exclusively regional language OTT platforms and 95 per cent of video views are not in English. Remixes of old Hindi film music are a favourite with even the likes of Coke Studio.

Increasingly, English words are being used in non-English conversations and 'Hinglish' is used alongside English. The most interesting use of English, however, is the use of the English script as the common script for writing text messages in any Indian language, despite each having its own script. Many Indians can speak more than one Indian language but do not know how to read or write the script. Equally many people do not speak or understand English well enough but almost all children learn the English alphabet in school, even if they are educated in a vernacular medium. Using the English script phonetically for all Indian languages therefore helps all around. It's not quite what Macaulay had in mind, but close enough, and yet another example of Indian ingenuity. *Achha idea hai na*? (Isn't it a good idea?)

Cuisine comfort and experimentation with Indianization

Even as Indian cuisine makes a big splash in new forms and flavours and brings cross-regional tastes to the table, the irrepressible Indian palate is driving the Indianization of every kind of Western cuisine. Even street carts and tiny eateries in small towns serve their version of Thai, Chinese, Tibetan, Mexican or Italian food. The latest is 'Sushi Do Pyaza', 'Daal Chawal Sushi' or 'Daal Chawal Arancini'.

Sameer Seth, creator of Bombay Canteen and O Pedro, two hugely popular restaurants in Mumbai, calls this phenomenon 'innovation with a touch of India'. He talks of familiar flavours in new forms and familiar forms in new flavours being the winning idea for cuisine. It is not unusual to see a signboard that says '100 per cent genuine Belgian Waffles—eggless, or a very lavish 'vegetarian only' feast at a very upper-income wedding that has haute cuisines of the world.

Nation pride: There is a personal positive rub-off on me if my country does well

I reported on a survey I did in 2016, in which we asked people the question, '*Acche din aaye hain kya?*' (Have good days come? As per the 2014 election slogan of the Bharatiya Janata Party of BJP, good days will come). A large number responded that good days had indeed come for the nation, though not for the youth or for themselves. Being a member of a country that can hold its own in the world and whose stock in the world is going up is like membership of a prestigious club, whose image does rub off on its members. Of course, the IT sector of TCS, Infosys etc. are to be given the credit for having started the transformation of India's image abroad, but they were very careful and skittish not to offend the foreigners (which made up their customer base) in any way. However, today's tonality body language and identity are at a totally different level.

Brand Orientation and Consumption Behaviour

'Imported' is no longer automatically better; 'Indian' is not automatically worse.

'Imported' was a magic word even until 2000. It automatically meant better and for premium brands, it added disproportionate consumer perceived value. Then came the Chinese invasion of the Indian market and imports by container loads from other countries, and imported goods of varying quality entered the Indian market. With the establishment of local offices and manufacturing by many global brands in India, and with the improvement in the quality of domestic offerings, the difference began to blur. Amazon is not seen to be a foreign brand by many because it is a marketplace that has so much Indian-made supply. Representative of the trend of comfort with Indian identity is the arrival of high-end Indian brands on the alcohol scene, priced higher in some cases than the most premium foreign brands. Pistola tequila is one example, popular with affluent young consumers. The Bombay Canteen has co-created the gin brand Greater Than, with the distillery Stranger and Sons, and the cocktail Perry Road Peru, a mix of pink guavas (perus) and gin. Artisanal and local high-end brands of cheese and craft beers are very popular in the Mecca of affluent youth culture, Bengaluru.

The country of origin or the question of local or imported is not a big brand value adder unless the brand demonstrates a value advantage over domestic brands.

Does Consumer India value brands?

I am often asked this question by foreign marketers new to India. All consumers value brands if they are genuine brands with deeply embedded positive values, have clear and likeable brand personalities and have made an effort to build a relationship with customers. Merely carrying a label that is famous elsewhere in the world does not add value to Indian customers by and large, except to a small segment of Indians who shop regularly around the world.

Retail brands at the moment have the high ground as far as brands in India are concerned—store brands; smaller, lesser-known brands and better-known brands all compete at e-stores. Small brands built on local social media have their niche following. Direct-to-customer (D2C) brands that have something that differentiates them or that consumers process as 'value adding' have been embraced, like Mamaearth in personal care, Paper Boat in beverages or HealthifyMe in fitness.

The basis for choice for Consumer India is still performance features and price.

Dearly Beloved, Ubiquitous Digital: Ringing in the New, Reinforcing the Old

Ring in the new

A lot already exists in the public domain about the enthusiastic adoption of all things digital by Consumer India, but no book on Consumer India can be complete without doffing a respectful and admiring cap to the digital revolution engulfing Consumer India. In my last book, I had a chapter called 'India's DQ or Digital Quotient' and made an observation that bears repeating. When temples have gone online and are live-streaming quite regularly, the digital era is here in full force and steeped in the veins of Consumer India. During COVID-19, during festival seasons, all big temples in Mumbai and perhaps elsewhere asked you to book your time slot and sent you an OTP on your phone, which you showed at the temple gate.

Modest-income consumers love digital ways of obtaining service because they provide status-blind service. Even if many can't do it on their own, there's a whole tribe of young digital middlemen who do it for you—facilitate medical treatment, help you avail e-governance, etc. You now get cheap and plentiful movies and banking services at your doorstep and money directly into your account for welfare benefits, and you can access more status-blind services than ever before for things such as booking a gas cylinder or a train ticket.

A testimony to Consumer India's embrace of the digital way is that the whole country, almost, learned to use a cell phone and WhatsApp, irrespective of literacy levels (low-priced smartphones from China and one of the lowest data costs in the world, as well as free digital payments, have undoubtedly spurred this). I love looking at WhatsApp display pictures of tailors, carpenters, shopkeepers, domestic staff, cab drivers etc. It tells you so much about them and their self-image—an expressive society gone even more expressive. He may not hold her hand in front of his mother but will certainly pose romantically for his WhatsApp display picture (DP).

Digital tools have added to the dignity and capability of even those not able to read and write. I had one man and two women who made up the domestic staff in my household. The man could read and write Hindi, but the women were both illiterate. I could not navigate a Hindi (Devanagari) script keyboard, and the man could not read English. Along came Google India with its transliterate feature, and I could send messages in Hindi, written in the Roman (English) script that would automatically get converted into the Hindi script. This liberated me—I could send long messages when I was unable to talk, and often asked him to convey them to the two women. The only trouble was that being the one receiving instructions from the boss, he started behaving like their boss, and that caused them a lot of stress, because they were actually doing more value-added work. Along came WhatsApp voice messages, and they quickly learnt to receive and send them and disintermediated him, taking back their own direct lines of communication and reporting relationships!

Also, with everything now operating via OTPs—which is by now a familiar word for all—the need to even enter passwords has gone. Biometrics has added to the ease for those not very literate.

Digital obviously saves costs and yet allows for a lot of style—videos of the couple with elaborate storylines and music, sent as wedding invitations, are very common and cost next to nothing and can be multilingual too.

Another interesting thing we notice is how digital interfaces are disciplining Consumer India into accepting rules. Anyone who is Indian knows that if a human being tells you that you cannot have something because no slots or seats are available or because you don't qualify, Indians will argue, bully and try and get their way. Switch to a computer, and there's no scope for argument and everyone just falls in line. So maybe we will eventually become a rule-obeying society, after all!

The Mumbai Police have an app where they post your e-challans now for traffic and parking violations, with a photo of your vehicle and location. The only thing to do is to pay up and not argue—there is no policeman to argue with and slip a hundred rupee note to. All travel bookings have gone online. If the computer tells you there are no tickets, or your preferred seat is not available, that's it. No more squabbling with the person at the counter, no more 'Do you know who I am?'. If the computer tells you that you are not eligible to do something given your fee category or membership category, there is no further argument. Government services have gone online, taxes have gone online and there's little room for everyday corruption and little room to hide wilful or accidental carelessness in tax matters!

Reinforce the old

Digital India is reinforcing the affiliative nature of Indian society even as greater income and exposure to the world are driving individualism. Nuclear families are the norm today. The whole clan weighs in virtually on wedding preparations, festivals are celebrated and new babies are monitored closely by many more family members scattered around the globe. Families and extended families are all on WhatsApp groups and even see pictures of what was served for lunch earlier in the day—it is as if everyone is living together in one large joint family! The smartphone with video calling and cheap data has been a boon to divided families and made consumer India even more affiliative a society than before. Indian mothers can flex their motherly muscles even more with their sons. There is a WhatsApp video doing the rounds pegged around India's moon mission, where the astronaut has just set foot on the moon when his mother calls (you see 'Ma' flashing on the screen) and says, 'Son, have you reached yet?'

The other thing that continually surprises me is how much religious content we have created and put on the internet, making our famed religiosity even more entrenched and easier to access. Live feeds from a range of temples are de rigueur.

You don't need to look for a priest—Google tells you how to conduct rituals. An enormous number of ancient religious texts are now online, with multilingual translations and multimedia, multi-modal renditions. I often wonder who on earth managed to digitize all these archives and upload them.

Ditto for the amount of Indian classical music uploaded online. There is no raga, no matter how rare, that you cannot find on the internet, no musician from the good old days whose recordings you cannot listen to.

Digizen India is the land of liberal and illiberal Indians. People sometimes think the internet is where the modern liberal Indian lives. But here's where every kind of illiberal Indian also lives, as you can see from the trolling that happens. The internet is entirely compatible with most other things that are hard to explain. A Naadi astrologer* now says, 'Scan your thumbprint and email it and we will tell you if your details can be found in the texts.' Matchmaking and dating have gone online, as have government records and special passes to cut lines at airports and so much more. Consumer India's central nervous system is truly the mobile smartphone powered by one of the cheapest data rates in the world.

Monster Consumers

Consumer India is probably one of the most demanding consumer bases in the world. It has gone through almost three decades of prices coming down and quality going up: first, on account of the transition from the socialist economy to the free market, when taxes came down and competition came in; next on account of Chinese goods and then the e-commerce revolution driving prices downwards and improving range and service (no-questions-asked returns, cash on delivery etc.); then the absolutely free digital payments environment.

---

* A school of astrology that identifies you today based on your name occurring in ancient texts. Not everybody is identified from the searches, though.

Along the way, before high touch could go out, hi-tech came in and 'omnichannel' and 'phygital' became the supplier's mantras. Monster consumers are shaped by the high-touch, hi-tech environment that suppliers offer them—you can go to an airport, stand in front of a check-in machine and as you fumble, have an airline representative come instantly to your aid. The security barrier is meant to open automatically as you scan your boarding card, but if you are too tired to do that, someone mans the barrier and will happily do it for you. The Uber driver doesn't want to always bother with using his GPS and will call you and ask you to guide him to your location.

My local vegetable seller with a cart across the road provides me exotic vegetables without my having to make an effort to go any further—I WhatsApp him my order before 5 a.m., and when he goes to the wholesale market, he fulfils my order (bespoke) and gets a high-value sale with no risk, while I get what I want with no effort.

Google Lens helps the freelance carpenter copy almost anything—he can aim, shoot, get detailed specs of furniture in designer showrooms or showrooms selling imported furniture at very high prices, and offer to make it at half the price!

And my registered mobile number will get me recognized with my data everywhere in person, at a call centre, or on the Internet—I don't see the need to keep track of anything myself. That is the sort of personalized service we Indians love.

Section II: Structure and Drivers of Heterogeneity in Consumer India and How to Think about Consumer Segmentation

Do we Indians have a penchant for projecting ourselves as an impossibly heterogeneous lot, whereas the reality is actually a lot simpler and not that different from other places? Yes, there are over a hundred languages, almost 20,000 dialects, and a mind-boggling array of food habits and cuisines. But aren't those differences melting and blurring in deference to the onslaught of modernity and the digital age? At the end of this chapter, I will leave the reader, especially the non-Indian reader, to decide.

The Many Forms and Faces of India's Heterogeneity

Outlier islands and heterogeneous mainlands

Consumer India is a creature that has lived over four centuries, and some or other section of it spans every point on the modern–traditional or ethnic Indian–Western global continuum. Behaviourally and attitudinally (throughout this chapter, the word attitude includes world view and values and is used interchangeably with mindset), Consumer India is highly fragmented. Some fragments are small islands of extreme behaviour and attitude outliers. We jokingly call one of them 'resident non-Indians' or RNIs (wordplay on 'NRI', the term for the non-resident Indian diaspora), a very Westernized group that see themselves as global citizens who just happen to have their main home base in India and live accordingly. At the other extreme is a small island of die-hard orthodox traditionalists, who believe that India is getting corrupted with new influences and they are the keepers and preservers of the *sanskaar* (the sacrament of the culture and manners and traditions of life that define us). Amazon knows this, and stocks both cow dung and quinoa. While traditionalists are a small group, diminishing in number with generational and environmental changes, there is a new small island, growing in pockets of India of young, aggressive defenders of the old ways.

There are several mainlands in the middle of the outlier islands, different from each other but with significant diversity within them. The North–South divide is one example of this, where demographics, personality and world view are so different. This divide stems from the totally different histories of the North and the South and the more recent historical influences that have shaped the mindsets of people in these two parts of the country.

Europe is often said to be a good analogy for this concept. But India's diversity and commonalities are far more complex.

India 1-2-3, or 'top half-bottom half India'

The chapter on structure showed that India has a thin top layer (on all demographic counts), a middle layer and a fat bottom layer. I sometimes think of it simply, using all indicators and anecdotes, as 'top half' and 'bottom half'. The latter comprises over 100 million households in underdeveloped rural areas, 40 per cent of households with virtually no savings and 20 per cent at the bottom who rightly qualify for welfare.

In contrast to this group, there is the top half, where less than great demographics are compensated by attitude and confidence levels, 'go-getting' levels and learnability levels, with the presence of some skill as a basis for earning. The top half can be interpreted as the 'arrived India' plus 'India already on the path to arrival', while the bottom half can be interpreted as 'still to get on the path of upward progress'.

Kishore Biyani, India's pioneering retailer who set up successful modern retail brands such as Big Bazaar and Pantaloons, called this divide the 'the aspirational class and the rest'. He, in fact, gave us the elegant conceptualization of India 1-2-3 as a means of thinking of broad homogenous segments of India. India 1 is the 'arrived', high-spending class, which is small and has aspirations and consumption similar in foundation to developed countries.

India 2 is the service class that makes life comfortable and in turn takes comfort from India 1—watchmen, lift-men, domestic help, nannies, drivers and many more. The incomes of India 1 are dependent on India 2. As most of us living in India and belonging to India 1 will attest, our earning levels and productivity are directly dependent on the support structure we have. Imagine an investment banker couple—their dependence on the nanny is extreme if they are to make their fat bonuses! India 2 also gains its advantages from India 1 in many ways—interest-free loans to manage their expensive life events and aspirations, jobs for children, other forms of advice and support, healthcare access when required, good-quality durables handed down, etc. It is a symbiotic relationship. India 2 also has its own network—the network of ward boys in a hospital gets India 2 better healthcare than India 1 can provide, as we saw during the times of COVID.

And then there is India 3, which is not linked or connected to India 1 in any direct tangible way and not even connected to India 2. This India lives a hard life with no surplus income, is vulnerable on many counts and often unable to give their children escape velocity to a new orbit, like India 2 can.

India 3 is the most vulnerable segment, but because of their large numbers, still has a significant consumption. However, this consumption is not stable, because their earnings are not stable. This group is made up of small subsistence farmers, landless labourers on daily wages, petty traders, and migrant workers with informal jobs and no skills. Yet this group does digital payments, which is the mainstay of some Hindustan Unilever brands and other brands like Parle Glucose. With increased efforts of rural financial inclusion, welfare schemes, health missions of the government and micro-insurance schemes, this group now has slightly more money than earlier, though finding work in bad economic conditions is still an issue.

However, as was discussed in the section on income trends in the previous chapter, the income of this group is steadily improving too on account of wage rates increasing and welfare schemes. Many of these families have family members who are migrants in big cities for at least a part of the year. This whole group we call Middle India; stabilizing its earnings and occupation will add significantly to consumption. The primary focus of this segment is to have a decent quality of basic necessities—a house with a roof and floor, toilets, schooling for their children, better food, and protection from debt traps from which they find it hard to climb out. Do they have cell phones? Many do, because this group has different income levels within it, with some being better off than others.

Regional diversity (Indian readers can skip this section!)

Indians are very familiar with the cultural divide between North India and South India, the Vindhya mountains being the demarcating line. People going from one to the other almost feel like they are in a foreign country. The food, language, traditions, and customs are all alien. While everything south of the Vindhyas is relatively similar, the subset of that—the four original southern states of Tamil Nadu, Andhra Pradesh, Karnataka and Kerala—is an even more homogeneous group. Telangana, a state recently carved out of Andhra Pradesh, is different from Andhra Pradesh on all demographic, economic and cultural factors because of its history.

And while, even within India, those in the south think of everyone in the north as a homogeneous group of 'Punjabis' and those in the north think of all South Indians as a homogenous group of 'Madrasis', there is significant diversity within each of these two broad regions. But again, within them, the languages and scripts are different in each, not even close to each other, and one can say the same for the politics. The calendars followed—lunar, solar or lunisolar—know no north–south boundaries and criss-cross the country with Tamil Nadu in the south, Bengal in the east and Punjab in the north having the same new year's day.

(Personal note: Growing up in Andhra, I was often told, 'Try not to marry a man from the north of the Vindhyas; you will not fit in'. They told me that I would have to learn to cover my head for traditional occasions, learn to eat wheat as a staple and not rice and learn to cope with what was stereotypically assumed to be a more aggressive and patriarchal society. Unless of course,

I married a man from Bengal in the east of India, which was stereotyped as educated and cultured and where women were treated as equal. But then, despite being raised with a vegetarian diet, I would have to start eating fish. My family used to also quip that there was no danger of my marrying a Kashmiri because my dark-skinned, relatively coarser South Indian looks would not compare well with the beautiful, fair, delicate Kashmiri women.)

I married a man from Maharashtra, south of the Vindhyas, who shared the same new year's day but had a 50 per cent overlap in terms of cultural rituals, and our mother tongues had different scripts but many of the same words. I learnt to eat wheat alongside rice as Maharashtra does, came to live in the teeming metropolis of Mumbai, where Gujarati food is the most popular vegetarian cuisine and Hindi has its own manufactured dialect called 'Bombay Hindi', and had staff, many of whom were migrants from Uttar Pradesh. We spoke English to each other as a common language of communication. Our daughter speaks English and her mother tongue, father tongue and Hindi. And yes, I did not marry the man from Bengal, but the family I married into had lived in Bengal for years, as my father-in-law worked in the coal mines of Bengal, and so we became a fish-eating household in the end!

Like all Indians, I have multiple identities—South Indian, Andhra, Maharashtrian, rootless cosmopolitan from Bombay, 'Mumbaikar' or of Mumbai and Mumbai-loving. I too, as a part of my identity, belong to other culture classes, as most Indians do, the concept of which will be discussed later in the section.)

In terms of consumption attitudes too, differences across regions of the country are clear and measurable, as any marketer will tell you. I once did a survey on what households across the country would do in situations of rising prices. How would they balance their budgets, what would they give up, and what would they keep? The findings, as expected, were very different between the north and south, driven by the different value systems. One would give up expensive baby powder for the baby (because no one is there to see what the brand is) but keep the almond biscuits, while the other would keep the expensive baby powder but give up bazaar-bought pickles and papads and instead make them at home.

Splintered identities: Not just different people, but many people inside one person too

A single Indian is also usually many different people valuing different things and behaving in different ways in different contexts. This is usual for all Asians, I am told—like Indians, they can be many different people and have no dissonance at all. Some cultures would call this hypocritical and inauthentic. In India, it is seen as adaptability (I suppose that is a good, pragmatic response to dealing with so much heterogeneity in one's life). In India, adaptability is considered a far bigger virtue than uniformity. After all, the gods changed character totally to deal with whatever situation they had to: the simple, the playful, the aggressive, the gentle—all representations of the same at different times, each celebrated for what it achieved.

A friend who is a member of the Tamil Brahmin community, which is considered pretty entrenched in its traditions and super-strong in its sense of identity, described himself to me as 'whisky–sambar', sambar being the traditional dish identified with the Tamil Brahmin community, whisky being considered the drink of choice of Westernized gentlemen. He said, tongue in cheek, that drinking single malt late into the evening was absolutely fine as long as he was able to get to the temple at 6 a.m. and sing Tyagaraja (a devotional music composer). In a very traditional, conservative Marwari family business, the daughters work in the business, not just the sons; it is not unusual to see them dressed in impeccable and edgy Western attire even as they conform to the other family rules of 'women must' or 'must not'.

Modernity has often been described in India as a 'negotiating tradition' or a 'tight fist loosening'. Where the points of negotiation are can and does vary from family to family, even within the same community or social class. 'The Me that I am when . . .' is a common and accepted formulation of behaviour. In fact, not being able to adapt widely is seen as a flaw, not a badge of authenticity.

Simple questions begetting multitudes of 'correct' answers: Incredible diversity of behaviour

In my previous life as a market researcher, I would frustrate my clients from less chaotic countries of the West by failing to give one clear answer to seemingly simple questions, such as 'What time do primary school children finish school in India' or 'what is the incidence of vegetarianism in the Indian population'. The first question depends on which state, what type of school and whether the school has a shift system or not in order to accommodate more children or more grades with their limited infrastructure.

The second question is best answered by the delightful WhatsApp meme on the subject, shown in Chart 1—vegetarian days of the week (which vary by the deity being worshipped), months of the year (holy months vs regular months), in-home versus out-of-home consumption of non-vegetarian food (now with the food ordering apps Swiggy and Zomato, non-vegetarian food brought from outside is acceptable, but cooked at home is not). Different communities also have different rules about what food is vegetarian—fish is not 'hardcore' non-vegetarian to some communities and individuals, and so on. If you are a pet food marketer, this question has a whole different, and equally complex, set of answers!

Chart 1: Answers to 'Are you non-vegetarian or vegetarian in your food habits?'

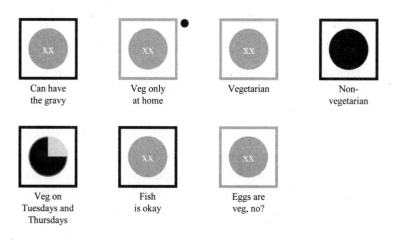

Can have the gravy	Veg only at home	Vegetarian	Non-vegetarian
Veg on Tuesdays and Thursdays	Fish is okay	Eggs are veg, no?	

How to Think about Market Segmentation of Consumer India

The impact of demographics

The usual demographic variables of income, occupation, community, and town class explain some of Consumer India's diversity to some extent; but as explained in the section giving the example of the north–south divide, groups defined by some demographic variables are different from each other but pretty diverse within themselves too. There is too little work available in India on clusters in terms of attitudes and values. Whenever done, they are done on small sample sizes (anything representative of all of Consumer India costs the earth) and usually restricted to the very low altitude pedestrian issues of buying behaviour and preferences—not at the people level, which can help determine why and what next.

This is a big reason why we are looking at a disturbing trend of marketers in India seeing marketing as data-led performance marketing, based entirely on auto-captured behaviour patterns. What do consumers do, and what makes them do it again? 'How many hits on digital properties do we need in order to meet sales targets?' is the most debated question, but how we improve the funnel through fundamental customer understanding feeding into marketing science is not really discussed. We see a greater competitive environment and diminishing returns from not digital engineering operational performance improvement. Perhaps this also explains the absence of brands not led by features alone. Consumer India's attitude and lifestyle heterogeneity are perfect for building brands differentiated by brand personality, but so far there are very few stereotypes being used that exclude more than they include.

Income is a big differentiator of behaviour and lifestyle but not of attitude. For example, as discussed earlier in this chapter, the aspiration to improve your own and your child's station in life cuts across all income groups. The goal is for the children to have one level more than what all parents have, to get at least one level higher. The specifics of what that 'one level higher' means varies by income level—to live in a flat and not a mud hut, to go to school and college, to have a set of material markers like a car and a big house and an 'office job', to go abroad and study and be a global citizen, as the case may be. Westernization or liberalism are correlated to some extent to education and the ability to travel overseas, but there is not necessarily a very strong correlation. The really rich just replicate their Indian lifestyles and limit their exposure to street influences even when travelling overseas. So do the traditional or the un-experimental group within the rich—there are overseas sightseeing tours that specialize in particular communities and carry cooks and own language-speaking guides along with them.

Town classes (metro, small town, rural, urban) do have differences in behaviour, but again, as was explained in the structure story, the differences are blurring, starting with income levels and total pools of money in each. Road connectivity, income distribution, digital and social and other media have blurred these attitude and behaviour differences to a large extent, though lifestyle (driven by supply as well) may be different. However, the 'villager' and 'city person' differences, which used to be very stark (as most Hindi movies of yesteryear used to show), are no longer so. Community living does put some brakes on the behaviour of young people in smaller towns and does not afford them the anonymity to be 'the me that I am when I am with friends', but again, with greater road connectivity, this difference is narrowing.

Age (young people) groups are heterogeneous too. This fragmentation also applies to the younger generation, something that we miss in all our discussions on millennials, Gen Y and Gen Z. India's young population has the same disparate characteristics as their parents. So they aren't all the tech-savvy, cool-dude individualist start-up folks that we think they are. They also are poor, ill-educated, rural, very badly want a government job with a steady income and are interested in marrying a good girl who will take care of their parents and also be their girlfriend (the last bit, that's what is new).

Occupation and education taken together are far better markers of homogeneity or heterogeneity, because, in some combinations, they form 'culture classes' that cut across income groups and population strata.

Culture classes: Homogeneous groups that exist within Consumer India

A good way for marketers to navigate Consumer India's heterogeneity is to think of homogeneous subgroups within it that are best called 'culture class', as in groups of people who have similar goals and/or mindsets and/or lifestyles and/or values and world views. Examples of some of the culture classes we see within Consumer India are briefly described in this section.

'IIT/IIM' culture class

This label is shorthand for a certain kind of person from a certain kind of milieu, who is part of a certain kind of social and cultural group of the elite. You often hear people telling a story about someone and describing the person as 'oh and he or she (usually he) is IIT/IIM'. This culture class comprises people who are typically from a variety of backgrounds, both affluent and not, elite and not. They are academically hard-working and bright, have worked hard and beaten stiff odds to do well in the competitive exams and get the ranks needed to get into these educational institutions. Ambitious, usually because of their conditioning, they are from homes where getting ahead the conventional way is demanded from children: hard work leads to good institutions of study, leads to good jobs, leads to social status and leads to being 'set in life', with all the trappings of arrival. Upper-middle-class and middle-class India is loaded with parents who make sacrifices and work hard to enable an IIT/IIM child.

A look at the IIT/IIM alumni over the years shows global achievers in all spheres, including the president of the World Bank, very successful tech entrepreneurs and CEOs of large global companies and so on. IIT is now a catch-all phrase for an engineering degree and IIM for a management degree from well-known brand-name colleges that are generally hard to get into.

Rich big business families from specific communities

This culture class, which is a very important segment for luxury, is an example of definite wealth and entrepreneurial smarts. They keep their traditional roots deep and alive through even today's generation, yet they embrace globally affluent lifestyles. They define the epitome of 'affluent India goes global on its own terms', with strictly vegetarian cuisine and large traditional weddings with exclusive global touches.

The start-up community

This culture class of entrepreneurs and aspirants are a growing swathe of India's youth culture, who come from all town classes, family income levels and educational levels. They are driven by ideas, and a desire to do something big and new not done before, and are ready to take the risk of not following the beaten track their parents would probably have liked them to take. The globe is their arena and the East and West hold equal attraction to them. Unlike generations before them of first-generation successful people, their Indian identity and experience are not a cross that they bear—they don't seem to feel the same need to adopt a 'Western' persona, even while their businesses are global. Situated in a large market opportunity that venture capital from around the world finds attractive, and citizens of a large and vibrant economy high up in world rankings, they don't baulk at marching into more developed markets. The last chapter talks in detail about of some their businesses—but from a culture class point of view, ideas like taking autorickshaws to Manchester (Ola), competing with Airbnb in China and America (OYO) or taking consumer electronics (wearables, BoAt) all over the world, represent a never-seen-before culture or class of Indians.

'Techies': IT and IT-enabled services workers

These are again young, and a distinct cultural class too. Working around the world or in India for the world, whether for Indian or global companies, many are from small-town India's numerous average-quality engineering colleges (this group does not qualify for the IIT/IIM culture class label), often being the first in their families to go to a far-off Indian city for work and then to go abroad and live abroad. They are confident of their capabilities (though narrow in range), very proud to be Indian, travel and live for spells in remote places around the world and see themselves as Indian global workers (as opposed to the global Indians). America is of course the place that they think of as their Mecca—talk to them, and you will hear frequent stories of how they were assigned to XYZ company in some distant part of the USA and how they solved a problem that the folks there had been unable to for many months. Very earnest, they are disciplined soldiers in a boot camp where following orders and being productive personally and in teams makes for good corporate citizenship and bonuses. They carry this over into their leisure too, it appears. I overheard a conversation once between two members of this tribe about a proposed safari holiday to Africa. They were saving to buy the best camera equipment, were going to photography classes to get the skills and then were going to embark on the holiday! They are a great consumer segment for holidays, experiences and weekend getaways; their identity and perks (gyms, food courts etc.) all come from their offices, which is why the lockdowns hit them hard.

The 'service' and 'business' culture classes

Ask middle-income people what they do, and the answer is usually 'service' (have a job and work for someone else) or 'business' (small entrepreneurs, usually.) These are two very distinct pan-Indian culture classes, with distinct world views and mindsets. For example, on the importance of education, risk-taking ability, how they process value from products and brands, and what they are ready to spend on and what they find wasteful.

The middle majority 'service class' of Indians

Usually in the upper one-third of urban Indian households (by income, between the tenth- and thirtieth-income percentile) across the country, they have a fair degree of cultural homogeneity. They describe themselves as 'ordinary' or 'middle class' people and go through life fairly contented though ambitious for their children to do well and be 'settled well'. A friend who went on to a popular matrimonial site to look for a match for her daughter summed it up by saying, 'The average Indian boy (from this stratum) is an engineer from somewhere small, perhaps with an MBA from an equally small college, is a vice president in a generally unknown IT company, has a mother who is a schoolteacher or homemaker, a sister who is married and works somewhere, maybe as a chartered accountant or equivalent and a father who works for a large public sector company or a small private sector one (in effect, has a steady job and is employed).' This is a hugely family-focused culture class, is focused on children/grandchildren and extended family, and they look forward to steadily improving their standard of living and retiring well. They live on the knees of middle-class comfort and are ambitious for their children but want them connected and not flying away to build their own lives, no matter how glamorous.

Indian small-business class

Another large cultural class is the small businessmen. They own shops or small factories and make a fairly decent living like their service counterparts, with vulnerability and volatility in the business (and income) being an accepted part of life. Today this group is buffeted by change. Forced to go 'legal' with paperwork and pay taxes, they are also facing a great deal of competition as the market economy becomes more vibrant and new types of competitors enter. Further, their children do not want to slog in small businesses (whose profit models do not work if owners do not spend 100 per cent of their time in the business) and want to move to higher-revenue, higher-investment and higher-risk models. Children of businessmen of this class usually become businessmen and typically do not have the mindset to work in a job. Their focus on making money and having the visible markers of success is as much as the service class, though the way they perceive and process value is quite different. Often, the difference between the modest surroundings of the business and the far more affluent surroundings of the home is quite sharp. This is a group in a lot of flux finding its identity, purpose and future at the same time.

'Working women' (in the top 60 per cent of the income pyramid)

Lower-income women are mostly forced to work outside the home to make ends meet. It is when a family is better off (top 50–60 per cent of the income pyramid) that not working outside the home becomes a social and family issue. Indians still use the phrases 'working women' and 'housewife' to distinguish women who work outside the home as opposed to women who stay at home (and probably work harder!). Working women or women who work outside the home are an interesting group comprising many cultural classes. Rena Bartos, author of *New Demographics: The Many Faces of the Women Market* (written in the mid-1990s), described two segments of working women as 'just a job' women and 'want a career' women. India has both and a third and growing group of 'earn from home' women who are home cooks, craftspeople, who buy and sell apparel, jewellery etc. out of their homes and so on.

Working women as a whole is a growing group, though a transient one—as women get older and take on family responsibilities, including children, and as families get richer, women tend to drop out and stay at home. The 'just a job' segment, however, far outweighs the 'want a career' women. The reason is, as has been well-documented, the many challenges that marriage and family still impose on women.

- *Householders:* A garment factory manager talked of the staggering high absenteeism among workers who were mostly women—they came from a social class where the money she made was desirable and appreciated but not essential (it was some version of Bartos' 'just a job' segment). He said if the husband's boss is coming home for lunch and chicken curry has to be made, she is told to take leave and cook. So too for festivals, family illnesses, social obligations and so on.

- *The 'not yet married' young women:* There is a cultural class of young women who are 'just a job' workers waiting to get married, filling in the time between completing their studies and getting married. This is a relatively new phenomenon in India, where it is assumed that young women will 'do a job', even if for a short while. Having certain kinds of jobs also makes young women more attractive in the matrimonial market, especially if they have a government job or a job that pays well but is low-stress and enables them to discharge all household duties while adding to the family income—at least until the children arrive.

What makes this group very interesting is that all of them suddenly have the income and the freedom they didn't have before. They know it may be short-lived depending on how their marital home is. But they do make hay while the sun shines, developing their outlook and personality and finding role models at this stage. They are also more likely to end up as CEOs in their new marital homes, especially if it is a nuclear family.

- *Home-based businesswomen:* There is another culture class of home-based businesswomen who have small businesses to augment the family income as well as their own and work from home. Very entrepreneurial and business smart, they are usually in businesses like crafts, apparel, jewellery and food services as well as in tuition classes and other such services that can be done from home.

- *Career women:* And then there are the career women who fit the mental model—be it in politics, government, teaching, NGOs, or business. I once had a 'senior statesman' business leader ask me why successful high-achieving women are so aggressive. I explained to him that, in India, in order to climb over all the family- and society-imposed hurdles—subtle, silent or explicit—from childhood onwards, women had to be aggressive. At every juncture, some would succumb and give up. Those who successfully navigated all hurdles are clearly tougher, demand more and are juggling more. They are overworked superwomen.

Own account workers

Another large meta culture class is 'own account workers' or solo service providers, as I prefer to call them. Within this group, there are segments by skill levels (hence needs, identities, income etc.), and many un-served needs exist for this segment. Academic and anthropologist Julien Cayla, in a paper called

'Recognition in India's New Service Professions', highlights a new set of service professions 'hailing from the lower middle classes doing "new services" work' (gym trainers, fitness home instructors, coffee baristas, bartenders in select upscale bars all over India, beauticians, speciality chefs) who interact differently and get respect from their English-speaking upper-middle-class customers.[3] A case study of the service company Urban Company, a two-sided platform for solo service providers of all kinds and households, quotes the service providers as saying how much more respect they have as a result of belonging here. A masseuse says that when the security guard of the building where her customer lived lewdly asked her if she would massage him as well, she haughtily said, 'Go to the app and register and we will see.' As elderly care becomes more required, given India's new silver population who do not have a family at home, nurses and ward boys also come through agencies with similar experiences and transformation. They learn and are trained—they are not household employees but professional agency employees and get treated very differently.

These are just a few illustrations of how different culture classes abound that determine consumer needs and behaviour that marketers can use to customize offers and build brands. Within each of these, there will be income subsegments, perhaps regional variations and finer differences.

Will Heterogeneity Decrease over Time?

We used to believe in the early 1990s that as India globalized, it would modernize, and as it modernized, it would homogenize. We are now proven quite thoroughly wrong. Our politics is now very regional and has been so for a while.

The internet, in fact, has made us even more heterogeneous. We are an affiliative, clannish, inquisitive, parochial society, with each of us having multiple identities and belonging to several reference groups, always seeking out 'people like us' like homing pigeons. WhatsApp makes all this easier and more efficient.

E-commerce now allows someone the capability and cost position to supply me exactly what I would have had if I had been in my home state, especially when it comes to food. As was discussed earlier, vernacular and regional languages flourish online, and more content is created in them now that there is an efficient way of getting a very wide catchment area.

So here's to making sense of the New India, even more bewildering and complex than the old India we had—we need to develop mental models of how India changes or we will drown in the sea of changes; we need to be prepared for the business and marketing complexity of a market of fragmented groups and splintered people who are monsters in their expectations and behaviour, being trained to become even more monstrous. Whether to search for similarities and stick with them or to pursue differences and address them is a strategic call that each business needs to take.

My mental model relates to how best to understand this increasing fragmentation and the common mega-trends and winds of change. The model is one of an archipelago: many islands floating in the same sea, subject to similar waves, but responding according to their own individual history and geography, their starting points and the strength of various tides and waves that touch them.

Section III: How India Changes and How to Read Change In Consumer India

Consumer India is complicated and full of contradictions. That is, of course, an understatement. But then, there are hardly any markets in the world that have had such high-speed change compressed over so little time and on economic, social, technological and political fronts. And none have had centuries, even millennia, of continuity of culture and tradition embedded in them. Consumer India changes in a multitude of tricky, underhanded ways. And so too is mapping the widespread and palpable change that has happened in the past two decades and is underfoot even as we speak—complicated and full of contradictions. This section will discuss how to read change and think about the bewildering changes and lack of changes that we see around us.

We know India has changed enormously. The trouble is that it changes in sneaky little ways, easy to miss even if you are carefully watching out for change.

This section is about how India changes, the dynamics of that change, how to read it, how to think about it and make sense of it, what shapes change in India and share some of the big changes that I think will shape the Consumer India of the future.

Today, rich young urban women are wearing much fewer ethnic clothes but rich young urban men are wearing ethnic clothes more often. Astrology and cows still reign supreme, but we have computerized horoscope casting and cow dung is being sold on Amazon (yes, all eight varieties of it, including organic cow dung. To the uninformed, cow dung is used as a purifier for religious rituals). Young people—Gen Z—are definitely dating more. Tinder is here and doing well, and premarital sex is par for the course. But Shaadi.com, Bharat Matrimony and Elite Matrimony still reign supreme. In fact, matrimonial ads today have changed too, but in interesting ways. Still wanted—fair, tall, Kayastha. But more specifications added on include 'MBA girl' or more specifically, 'an anaesthetist bride for doctor boy', whose family owns a nursing home. And what's changed, surprisingly, is that she doesn't need to be an expert or even a competent cook. WhatsApp, where all the great Indian truths now reside and are embedded into society, has a wonderful cartoon. Two sets of parents are arranging a match, when the bride's parents unabashedly say, 'She can't cook, but she can order online.'

The best metaphor for the sneaky and complex change in Consumer India, I find, is in women's clothes. While we are so busy watching for clues in the size and rate of growth of the women's Western wear market (and shops have started to put up signs 'Western women's wear (sic) available here'), the real action has been happening on the sari, the blouse and the salwar kameez. Google and this is what you get.

The sari is being draped in bold and innovative new ways (no, the stitched sari, ready to wear is not all that common, though it would have been a logical and expected way for the sari to 'evolve') and blouses have gone from boring or daring to stunning—and different—to functional (crop tops for blouses that work with pants too).

The kurti, both the word and the genre of the garment, appeared after 1991. A mid-thigh to knee-length kurta (tunic), it is perhaps the best supplier response to the desire for modern attire for India's consumers and their not-very-open-minded families or society or even themselves.

Another example of how India changed is in its politics. The two opposing poles are clear now and here to stay—the BJP and the Congress, the earlier two dominant parties have now become the NDA and the UPA (now re-branded to INDIA), the constituents of which are ever-changing from election to election. But we do see the dynamics of change very clearly—single-party dominance is mostly out, an alliance is in, and merger and acquisition-type politics are in (who allies with whom decides who gets to rule at the state and the centre). Enemies in the state, friends at the centre—this flip-flop behaviour is here to stay. Some old patterns are evergreen, while some are mostly gone forever.

So how do we make sense of all these changes occurring simultaneously? Looking at a large list of changes is very confusing. We see bits and pieces of trends, and we are tempted to ignore counter-trends that spoil our story. Sometimes, we look only at a few changes and not at the larger list of changes and have the niggling worry that we aren't doing our jobs well enough as business and marketing people to counter threats from the environment that affect our businesses and to consider all the opportunities that come with change.

The challenge of the Indian market is to develop a mental model of how India changes, and how to read it and understand it. Let me share my mental model with you.

Mental Model of Change 1: Morphing versus moulting change

One part of the mental model relates to understanding the 'everything seems to change but nothing seems to change' nature of Indian attitudes, mindsets, social norms, etc. Social attitudes in India change in a slow and morphing way—slowly from within, but steadily and definitively, hard to recognize and see because we are looking for moulting change like a snake that sheds its skin, and we keep searching for evidence of the skin and getting disappointed.

Indian society doesn't moult—it morphs. So attitudes go from being very traditional to somewhat traditional to somewhat modern to modern and then discontinuously on to ultra-modern. All this happens differently in different pockets and different facets. So the traditional daughter-in-law from an orthodox community will be well-educated, will be allowed to have a small business of her own, wear Western clothes with no restraint and yet not be able to leave the house, whether for an evening out or a short vacation, without permission.

Mental Model of Change 2: 'This as well as that'

When thinking about change in India, we know that it is never 'this or that', but it's always 'this *and* that'. We have not shed a single deity in our pantheon, but we have added a new one, in keeping with the changing times—there is a Dalit temple to the Goddess English, as reported in a newspaper some years ago with an accompanying photograph. We have not shed a single channel of shopping. The vegetable vendor down the road, the *kirana* (local grocer), the supermarket, and e-commerce are all added to our portfolio of places from where we shop. No wonder all retailers say that they plan to go omni-channel.

Mental Model of Change 3: Tipping point, not sudden pivoting

My third mental model of how India changes is the tipping point way of change or, to use an Indian idiom, not *jhatka* (at one stroke) change but *halal* (slow bleed or slow burn). The language of mega-trends is often not the language of India. Often, momentum builds as a result of creeping trends; example being very slowly increasing levels of income that finally create financial surpluses (and the ability to save) for most households. Or the way food expenditure creeps down and non-food expenditure creeps up. Or the way the number of years of formal education per person creeps up or the differences between urban and rural get blurred as people slowly move out of agriculture, and villages morph into census towns, that twilight zone between urban and rural. Or the way agriculture has now become feminized as the men have moved on to the nearest cities and the women are tending to farms.

Another form in which the tipping point is reached is what I have described in my earlier books as the change wave, coming as a confluence of little changes occurring simultaneously, each insignificant by themselves but collectively forceful. In the case of the powerful change wave of the rise of women in India, it is a bunch of creeping changes that have come together—legal changes such as inheritance laws, reservations in political and business arenas, the need for a second income as family aspirations rise, the increasing number of years of education, the practice of working a few years before marriage—to create a huge change wave.

Mental Model of Change 4: Large mass, a small acceleration

My fourth mental model relates to the different ways in which the force of change is brought about. We know from physics that $F = M \times a$ (force is equal to mass multiplied by acceleration). In India, the same force is generated in two ways: by a large mass of people changing with a small acceleration and by a small mass of people changing with a large acceleration. Usually, people associate the force of change with high acceleration and don't quite realize the large force of change and its attendant opportunities that a large mass moving slowly can bring about. Examples of this are changing buying and spending patterns of the poor, an increase in access to public goods, financial inclusion and the rise of the value of the rural market, or how the large body of women, changing a little bit each, is transforming the way Consumer India thinks. Examples of small masses changing at high speeds are what are wickedly called urban RNIs, (resident non-Indians), rich Westernized urban families, the youth of the top 10 per cent in terms of income in large cities who are the offspring of well-heeled parents—they rarely cook at home, they take exotic holidays, have interesting jobs and follow their passion of the day. It is not unusual for parents of this group to say, 'We spent crores on his Ivy League MBA, and now he has decided to be a pranic healer in Portugal.'

It Takes Two to Tango: Suppliers Change Consumers Too

So much of the discussion on how markets change assumes that it is customers who drive change as they evolve by making the consumption choices that they do. The fact is that so much of consumer evolution has to do with how suppliers shape it. Markets and consumers, for example, become more sophisticated even as the middlemen get sophisticated. The supply environment of digital facilities made available to consumers, for example, created a digitally savvy Consumer India.

The next section of the book is on supply and discusses how supply is changing India.

5

Demand Leads,
Supply Lags

Consumer India is still underserved and supply lags behind demand.

While there has been a tsunami of new supply in the past three decades, most of it is small-scale supply or opportunistic imports. The good news is that there are enough avenues for value addition, and the market is still wide open. The consumer is saying '*yeh dil maange more*' (my heart asks for more)—more real brands, more customer-centricity in addressing my needs.

However mass markets do not wait and are seeing new, improved action from small physical and e-commerce supply and new digital business models, though not at a large scale. It truly is the land of Lilliput where the small are collectively capturing and powering large parts of the market.

Mapping the Supply Landscape in Relation to the Demand Environment

The Structure of Supply So Far

Despite India's large and steadily growing private consumption ($2 trillion in 2023) and the fact that India has the largest consumer base in the world of young, keen-to-consume people, its supply environment lacks the heft commensurate with the opportunity. It is still an underserved market, both in terms of quantity and in terms of range and variety of supply.

Big boys not flexing their muscles

The problem with the Indian market has been that barring the top of the pyramid, it has been much too challenging to create consumer-acceptable supply at consumer-affordable prices and make a profit doing so. It has required huge amounts of innovation, long payback periods and managing a risky business that has razor-thin margins and very high volumes. Therefore, for many large companies, both multinational and Indian, most of India's consumer market opportunity has not constituted an immediately addressable market but a 'watch this space for when it is ready' distant horizon.

Multinational corporations (MNCs) have not deployed their full global might in their India business for a variety of reasons to be discussed in the next chapter, starting from their dominant logic about how markets evolve to their strategic intent—getting incremental revenue from India as an extension market for what is already available elsewhere versus building a new 'made for India' business by leveraging global competencies and knowledge. The turnovers of many of them are embarrassingly small when compared to the years spent here. Notable exceptions are of course a handful of old economy companies such as Maruti, Samsung, HUL and the new breed of Amazon, Google, Facebook and some newer economy businesses. On the other hand, several large domestic companies across a variety of sectors have also not invested in serving all of Consumer India, preferring instead to focus on going abroad to build the Indian multinational or be the Indian back office and knowledge services provider to the world, offshoring whatever is possible. Given the exchange rate, earning in dollars is a better deal than earning in rupees, and serving richer markets is better than serving poorer ones. Some sectors like pharmaceuticals have focused equally on both.

A study of the top 200 listed companies in India by turnover, filtered further by B2C presence and the number of similar-sized companies there are in each sector (extent of choice available to the consumer), shows slimmer pickings than expected. The largest consumer-facing company, a telecom company that serves all of Consumer India across all geographies and the income pyramid, has a domestic turnover of around $11 billion. Against that, there are just two large fast-moving consumer goods (FMCG) companies with a turnover of about $6–8 billion who also straddle all geographies and the entire income pyramid, although one of them is predominantly a cigarette company. In the next tier, there are a clutch of five FMCG companies in food and personal care at between $1.5 and 2 billion. One mass-market grocery retailer is just short of $4 billion, as is a jewellery and watches retailer with its own brand. There are two two-wheeler retailers, the lifeblood of private transportation, who are at about $4–5 billion in revenue including exports, and one healthcare provider at under $2 billion. Clearly, there is a lot more room for more large companies to serve Consumer India. The enormity of India's steadily growing private consumption expenditure and its continued large share in India's GDP, and the fact that Consumer India has the largest, youngest, most consumption-desiring population in the world, has not yet attracted the commensurate investment and focus that it should have.

The land of Lilliput

As a result of the limited presence of large companies, small suppliers and small trading importers have occupied a large share of the market in most sectors. The small-scale sector in India contributes to over a third of India's manufacturing output. They offer over 30,000 brands, and many of these are in FMCG, consumer durables, cosmetics, packaged food and other B2C segments, serving 80 per cent of the population and working through twenty million retail outlets. This is about ten times more than the 3000 brands estimated to come from the large sector. The bulk of the Indian market is indeed the land of Lilliput, with small suppliers serving small (low-income low per-capita consumption) buyers. Even the B2B business is best characterized as B2B or b2b.

These small suppliers are regional in nature, with thousands in number in every sub-region of the country. They straddle all categories and have varying degrees of brand strength and loyalty. At every price point beneath the nose of the large companies, these products carpet-bomb the Indian market. While many of them operate with a herd mentality and are clones of each other, collectively, they are a formidable group of very fast followers, reverse engineering (copying) the latest from abroad and able to latch on to trends very fast. Their learnability is also very high. If blinds are replacing curtains, they know how to do that; if house cleaning needs an understanding of new materials, they can do that too. Using Google Lens, they can copy furniture and home accessories from a big store. They can figure out how to fix the ever-newer models in electronics. The WhatsApp joke floating around when Tim Cook visited India says it all—it gave his schedule and said meeting with the prime minister, then inaugurating a new Apple store in a large, swanky mall, then meeting the chief minister and then a trip to a local market to meet a local chap who will demonstrate how to unlock an iPhone for Rs 150.

A significant number of small businesses do more sophisticated innovation and occupy large market spaces that large companies don't, or manage to do it cheaper, better and more relevant to customer needs than large companies. This applies to high-tech sectors like IT products and services and relatively more everyday products like apparel, certain kinds of durables and appliances and food, in particular. The traditional Indian jewellery market of precious metals and stones has been taken by storm by thousands of small suppliers with designs that are quite amazing and prices that are a fraction of the real thing. Earlier called costume or imitation jewellery, they now tellingly call themselves fashion jewellery, and do a wide range from very 'authentic' replicas of real 'locker jewellery' (as in, precious jewellery usually to be stored in bank lockers) to service destination weddings, to doing beautiful designs in ordinary metal or silver with one gram of gold plating for those who don't want to wear ordinary metal. The prices range from throwaway prices that all sections of society can afford of Rs

100 onwards, going up to Rs 20,000 or so, still one-tenth of the real thing and just as beautiful. As the Clairol hair colour advertisement in the old days used to say, 'Does she or doesn't she? Only her mother can tell.' It is not unusual to walk into a designer apparel boutique and find that bridal wear outfits cost Rs 2–3 lakh apiece, but the jewellery accessories are just Rs 2000 at most.

Taken together, the quality of the small businesses straddles a wide range, from poor to 'does the job very well' to 'more appropriate and better value than large company supply' (because they customize better and strip down over-engineered features and cost from the 'global' offers, etc.).

I once had a meeting with the visiting executive board of a very prominent American food company. Their conference room display was bare—they only had a few packaged products from similar big global companies, and this view of the market gave the appearance that the market was yet to experience a supply revolution. I took with me a sampling of products from the food shop across the street that stocks hundreds of packaged snacks, both sweet and savoury, as well as ready-to-eat Indian breakfast options in retort pouches, all made by small-scale suppliers, and all at very good price-performance points. Needless to say, it was dismissed as 'not our competition'. There is a small company that has created a competitor for the Indian market to the global leader Salesforce, and another that has a product for managing security in large apartment complexes similar to security systems offered by large global companies like Honeywell; both are at much lower prices for equivalent performance than their global competitors. The after-market for auto ancillaries and electronics is also dominated by small suppliers who offer good quality and original parts replacement at a far lower cost and far quicker service. Many of the small businesses are actually micro businesses that, so far, have done better on customer-perceived value as compared to large companies. Had Intuit been able to adapt its products and pricing to the Indian market and been more patient, it would have had a very large business indeed from the small suppliers, many of whom are extremely hungry for more.

The Chinese invasion and opportunistic imports

Just like everywhere else in the world, the Indian market is also served by a large influx of products from China that have been specifically made for India. I visited a handloom sari weaver in the hinterland of Andhra Pradesh several years ago, and he said that he had spent the last month in a remote province in China. He said that he had been invited to spend a month and show them what patterns and colours of weaves worked in the Indian market so that they could replicate them in wonderfully vibrant and appealing synthetic printed saris made for India. Saris from China come at unbelievably low prices, and there are no takers in the lower-income groups for silks that are cumbersome to maintain. Never before have modest-income, mid-to-low-income consumers been better dressed or had so much variety to revel in. The influx of Chinese goods has given Indian consumers never-seen-before products or familiar products at a quality–price equation that they never dreamed was possible—apparel, fabric, accessories, footwear, plastic boxes and bottles, to name a few.

There are never-seen-before products like battery-operated fairy lights and diyas of a quality that has been hitherto unaffordable by the bulk of Indian consumers. It is the same with blankets, rainwear, footwear, stationery, umbrellas, school supplies for children, table mats, hairpins, and so on. Even idols and Indian-style jewellery come from China. The mass market in India is served by China and the widespread wholesale channel takes these everywhere, deep into the hinterland.

There are several other sources of small traders importing products opportunistically from wherever available, including the very highly-priced fresh fruit and premium packaged food that serves the upper class in large cities.

A lot of this unbranded supply imported by small and large trading houses simply comes on a consignment basis, so, as a consumer, you take what's available and if you choose to purchase something you liked again six months later, the brand or product may not be available. This also applies to large mid-market, modern retail stores that also source imported goods opportunistically, which is why if you go back for repeats of the products you liked, there are no guarantees that you will find them. While this may fly in the face of retail management theories, Indian consumers, especially in the lower income groups, find that the sheer joy of discovering what's available elsewhere in the world adds far more value to consumers than the ability to make repeat purchases!

The new small-business digital ecosystem—marketplaces and small e-tailers

The digital revolution has created a new set of marketplaces for small suppliers, the leader of which is, as expected, Amazon. Several wannabe Amazons have now come up with varying levels of category specialization. Whether many of these newer marketplaces offer value-added services or are just digital real estate is left to be seen. It reminds me of the nineties when so many physical malls were built by real estate developers and not retailers, and most did not have the magic that malls everywhere else in the world did.

India has missed a widespread large mall and physical retail chains revolution[1] as it leapfrogged to the digital world and embraced e-commerce. I have often said that everyone has been working for the well-being of e-commerce. The government of India helped with pathetic potholed footpaths even in the most moneyed localities, the traffic helped, the lack of parking everywhere helped, as did the ineptness of sales staff.

So, the crowded markets of India with small shops are now a crowded online space, with even more small shops—the crowded land of Lilliput Indian marketplace prevails even more, as small digital shops mushroom because they need even less investment than physical ones.

The e-revolution has also caused the mushrooming of a lot of social media-based products—let's call them boutique, designer or chef labels—and Instagram is full of them. As logistics services and digital payment gateways have developed, the number of small e-tailers has increased exponentially. All the high-street stores that used to offer home delivery earlier now have e-commerce front ends as well.

There is, in the FMCG space, an explosion of new brands that call themselves D2C even though many of them go through e-retail marketplaces and have built revenue and customer loyalty to varying degrees. There are an estimated 800 D2C brands today with a combined turnover of $4 billion.[2] It is now a crowded space of 'Lilliput brands', with the personal care space alone having eighty and fashion having many more. Some of the more successful ones have built revenues of Rs

100 to 300 crores in three to five years. Funded by private equity, D2C brands have built a foothold with innovative and differentiated offers but they now find that in order to build on the momentum and achieve a much bigger scale, they need to scale the conventional way. Venture capitalist Kanwaljit Singh, a former Hindustan Unilever marketer, who has funded many prominent D2C brands, is very bullish about the future of D2C brands in the large, underserved and digitally friendly consumer base that India has. However, he also says that it is hard to build a strong brand and scale without a physical presence in retail and without money spent on communication and advertising. 'The cost of customer acquisition is the main issue. It is broadly 2X higher now compared to the initial phase of D2C of 2015-16.'[3]

So, while retailers have an online presence, e-tailers now seek varying degrees of physical presence as well. The omni-channel profusion of the land of Lilliput is now complete.

What's wrong with small-scale supply? Consumers in India would benefit a lot more if the segments of small supply that are the brightest and the best could scale and be a formidable and ubiquitous force that serves them. Today, the best diamonds in the dust are discovered by consumers because someone told someone about it or by endlessly tracking Instagram and reading reviews; surely there can be a better way for good supply to scale and grow from strength to strength? What's stopping them now is access to patient and reasonable finance and know-how on how to go about scaling businesses. The better ones get venture funding and the know-how and linkages to grow, but many do not even know how to go about this.

The new-economy digital business models that will reimagine and redefine the future of India's supply

The most exciting new developments which will be discussed in detail in the later sections of this chapter are the new business models that the digital world has made possible and how they may actually be the long-awaited messiahs of the mass market. They are able to square the circle of consumer affordable prices and supplier profit, which MNCs and large Indian businesses hesitated to do or could not because of their high-cost basis and mindset.

Large companies have traditionally been at the forefront of the development of consumer markets in emerging markets because they have the resources, the capabilities and the resilience to invest in innovation and R&D to add value to consumers' lives. But now the bar is getting higher for creating consumer-perceived value advantage in India.

Consumer India Is Still Underserved and Supply Lags behind Demand

There has definitely been a tsunami of new supply of all kinds compared to 1991 or even pre-2000. Quality and quantity of products have seen a quantum jump, in terms of both familiar products and never-had-before products that have delighted consumers. However, India is still an underserved market on many counts—the quantity of decent supply relative to its enormous potential, availability of differentiated offerings for diverse segments of consumer needs and a range of consumer pain points and consumer needs that are left unaddressed.

It is not that supply has not ramped up, but that consumption readiness and consumer sophistication have ramped up faster. Even as we celebrate new supply, the scale of India's consumption is something that businesses still need to wrap their heads around as they review their investment and growth appetites. The late management guru Prof. Sumantra Ghoshal used to say that companies have to win three battles—the battle for dreams, the battle for markets and the battle for competencies. In India, dreaming big is not a hallucination or an aspiration— the underlying demand justifies it, provided of course the price-performance point is right. We are constantly surprised at how much demand gets unleashed when appropriate supply shows up. Had the telecom rates not been what they are, we would not be the largest internet-using population in the world, and that too with just 50 per cent internet penetration today. Had digital payments not been free and the public good of UPI not been there to force interoperability and kill closed loops, had there not been a Paytm leading the charge with enrolling small street vendors, later boosted by GPay joining the fray, India would not have had the largest number of digital transactions in the world.

The digital payments revolution is one example of how, when the offer is compelling (in this case free too), the response is huge, as with cell phones and smartphones, WhatsApp usage, online entertainment and the enthusiastic embrace of Chinese goods.

It's the same demand unleashing that we see and marvel at with just one big low-cost airline, Indigo. While their new order from Boeing for 500 new aircraft, the largest order in the world, causes many even in India to gasp 'Where on earth . . .', the truth is that everyone wants to fly. Driving across the country is uncomfortable, time-consuming and nightmarish if you are using public transport. Indian roads are not like those in America. I used to marvel at how in America you could take a cup of coffee and drink on your drive without scalding yourself. Try even drinking water in a moving vehicle on an Indian road. Many more low-cost airlines and flights connecting all parts of the country will be lapped up. The doorman in an apartment block in Mumbai on leave to see his family in Varanasi does not want to waste his precious family time and wants to fly. So does the bellboy in a small hotel in Ahmedabad going to his family in Guwahati. It takes him three days either way by train. His holiday is for three weeks. Yet as of today, even newly built airports are running out of capacity and already have mile-long queues just to enter on most days. The fact that people in the south of India are early risers and India is a young country hits you hard as you navigate the queues in Chennai airport at 5 a.m. on Monday or Friday.

Truly affordable housing and mortgages to support purchase is a bottomless pit of demand. Even luxury housing in South Bombay or assisted-living facilities anywhere have room for a lot more supply, given more children living abroad, starker differences in lifestyle between generations and so on.

A trip to any developed market, in the East or West, makes one wonder at the plethora of problem-solving products available. The landlord won't let you put nails in the walls. Here's how you can hang heavy paintings. Baby products are beyond imagination—a friend's daughter bought a baby 'shusher' that makes shushing sounds (for my generation, raised socialist for the better part, this seems a bit excessive but nevertheless useful for an exhausted new mother with a difficult baby and no support system). For a country that has almost 25 million babies a year, and with so many households having children and being so fiercely education-focused, one would have expected hundreds of real brands of children's toys and expect them to be highly differentiated too. There ought to have been several children's channels in each language, several tiers of branded toy stores—'branded' not being labels with awareness (also most 'brands' in India are but 'who am I, why buy me, what do I do for you' businesses that are sharply defined and that live the chosen proposition). Even during COVID, when suddenly all rich and poor children had to take up online education, there was no sudden rush of low-cost, simple tablets that could just do the one job that needed to be done and in a size that could hold the child's attention. The online education world is now here to stay, but low-cost simple 'gets the job done' tablets, customized for this purpose, are yet to appear.

Till IKEA came to India, despite hundreds of thousands of talented local furniture craftsmen who were very capable of replicating most things from anywhere in the world, no local retail brands of furniture emerged which were not restricted to a few cities and a few locations and so cloned. There are just a handful of large chains of good apparel brands like everywhere in the developed world that have a distinct brand proposition, personality and design language to back it up. There are thousands of apparel labels, but many are a motley collection of what is generically called 'ethnic wear' or 'Western wear'.

The food category is a great example of enormous vibrancy on the street of all kinds of food and continuous innovation around it both in content and form. There is also enormous vibrancy in regional pockets of hyper-local brands. But other than Amul and some brands in the dairy cooperative sector and some national biscuit companies with multiple brands, we haven't seen much from the large, organized sector. India is sadly the diabetic capital of the world, but we haven't seen even a handful of diabetic-friendly good brands on a national scale.

This is true category after category. There are several amazing companies making fashion jewellery, as we discussed earlier, but a handful of real brands and fewer with a national footprint.

All of India is short of electricity, and most urban homes have inverters (battery systems that feed electricity to the house during power outages). Yet there is no big national brand of inverters with a clear product–market fit, and consumers are at the mercy of several small providers, with no basis to gauge their credibility or competence to advise on configurations, no price uniformity and little or no maintenance service. Every electrician in the locality says he is an inverter expert. Similarly, generators do not sit well with rising eco-consciousness, reliable solar providers of national repute and excellent advisory, design services and maintenance are hard to come by (same story as inverters) and there is no one thinking of holistic solution systems. As rich India buys more and more second homes, the potential is enormous. More so because much of India also lives in small independent homes, not in condominiums. And on low-cost solutions for modest-income consumers, all one needs is a light and charging station per room so children can study, and dinner gets cooked.

One would have expected several brands of ready-to-eat or heat-and-eat chapatis. While there are some good ones available selectively (mostly in rice-eating South India, where wheat is a 'foreign food'), it is surprising that ready-to-cook chapatis haven't become the default option all over India, despite women getting to do more outside the home and cooking help getting harder to find. Consumer durables to automate the house are the most sought-after household productivity gadgets. Yet there are no well-penetrated large-scale consumer durable chains with allied services—city-specific and state-specific chains do exist, but not everywhere, and national chains like Croma are few and far between in tier 1 and 2 cities, despite the income share by geography data that we have seen. Get off a plane at the swanky airport at Coimbatore—an affluent city, the sixteenth largest urban agglomeration in India and at the crossroads of textiles, light engineering, tourism, and home of new-age big brand spiritual gurus and new-age retirement homes—and if you find that you have left your phone charger at home, there is no electronics accessories chain you can duck into and buy one. You need to go into the city to one of the two Cromas to get one. Second-hand and refurbished electronics and durables have very big opportunities, and small retailers do trade-ins very happily. But there are no large organized, national or even regional well-penetrated brands or chains when, in fact, there should be upwards of at least five or six, given the opportunity.

Sari blouse tailors are a diminishing breed, and sari wearers are more occasional wearers than regular wearers. The young wear crop tops with saris and are very happily liberated from the tyranny of tailoring. At last, there are ready-made blouses available, but those of us familiar with this garment that is particularly troublesome to fit know that it takes a lot of different styles and cuts and hence needs many stock keeping units (SKUs) to really make this work, not to mention material and colours.

There is a brand of stretch leggings and trousers in knitwear that was mentioned in earlier chapters: GoColors. They have opened over 500 stores in 120-plus cities, and the speed with which the needle has moved for consumer adoption of 'bottom wear' yet again tells the story that relevant supply can stimulate demand. Doing the same thing for knitwear sari blouses would boost the category as well, but there are no takers yet. Just as there are no takers to set up small beauty parlour chains all over small-town and peri-urban/rurban India, where survey after survey shows that beauty parlours and their services are very much in demand.

There are many places that I can go to buy a diamond ring, but I remember having an 'aha' moment in this category when my daughter got engaged and found that her ring was loose. I had just landed in Boston, and I was telling a friend of mine this, and she said, 'Oh, let's go to a jewellery store.' And sure enough, they had a solution to this problem—a little band clipped to the ring to create a 'false bottom' and secure it. Of course, they even had variants and asked for 'silver or non-silver', meaning $100 or 10! But that is a consumer society. It's not the first time an engagement ring has been too loose, and someone noted the problem and found a solution.

One Urban Company (offers a very wide range of home and personal care services), and one Nykaa (cosmetics e-tailer and retailer) are not enough for a market like India. They are tokens like flagship stores are, and their small turnover versus the large demand and large consumer base rests the case that much more effort and investment are needed in being customer-centric. Several online offerings in various categories are merely 'Crawford market on the net', i.e., marketplaces with no responsibility for value-added services (that's why Amazon has so much traction with Consumer India).

One characteristic of the state of supply in India is that it is fragmented and has several small players. The other is that there are miles to go even for so-called category leaders to go beyond the basic product and offer value-added services that consumers desperately want (what Theodore Levitt called the augmented product).

The Good and the Mixed News

The good news about India's consumer market is that it is still wide open. Even the apparent oligopoly in many sectors is because the era of competition is yet to reach full bloom. The other news, good for consumers and not so good for established suppliers, is the enormous surge in the variety of new supply using digital business models. Admittedly, most are some way off in their path to profitability and still small but show the promise of cracking open the mass market by having business models that give the consumer acceptable quality at affordable prices as well as a profit to the supplier.

There is no clear demarcation that rich customers will use big company supply while modest income consumers buy small company supply. Competition in any consumer segment can come from all tiers and types of supply. Consumer India has always used a portfolio of products—in the beginning, it was essential to balance the budget, then later, as incomes grew, it was the joy of discovery as well as the fact that Indians are almost schizophrenic in how they live (the 'me that I am when . . .' discussed earlier), with various shades and grades of habit, modernity and tradition mingling.

So, as the iconic line from an oft-quoted Pepsi ad said, 'yeh dil maange more', the (consumer) heart demands a lot more supply, of course at price-performance points that customers will accept.

The next section on supply will deal with issues related to this:

- Why have MNCs not been able to win in India so far and is the tide turning on this?

- What strategic posture are large Indian companies taking in serving their home market?

- Learning from innovations that India has seen that have been capable of getting the job done well and at prices and profitability that work for both customers and suppliers— whatever happened to these innovations?

- What kind of new-economy digital business models are coming up (an illustrative analysis of some unicorns from India), and why can they crack open the Indian mass market better than anyone has done before?

THE FUTURE OF INDIA'S CONSUMPTION

 Consumer India Structure Story

 Consumer Behaviour Story

 Supply Side Story

6

Passage through India: The Multinational Journey and Lessons Learnt

Making a serious dent in the Indian market requires MNCs to design 'made for India' businesses that may be quite different from what they have in the rest of the developed world. They have resisted doing this for many reasons, including mindset, governance, faulty dominant logic and perceived risk. As a result, most MNCs have struggled in India. MNCs should leverage their global competencies and knowledge and design 'made for India' businesses—keep the religion, change the ritual.

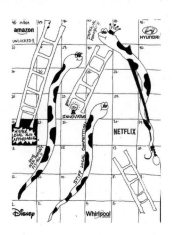

Chant the Mantra 'India Is Different'

It is by now well-documented that MNCs, especially from the Western, developed market world, have not done well in India.

When the big global consulting companies set up shop in India in the 1990s, they stridently said that it was only a matter of time before global corporations from the West entered the country, rendered existing Indian business models obsolete and modernized and globalized India's markets, just as they had done everywhere around the world. From the mid-1990s until about ten years ago, whenever I said that the Indian market would evolve differently and would never follow the evolutionary paths that Western developed markets took, requiring custom-built strategy to address it, there was scepticism and derision from the global consulting high priests who said that we in India did not understand the nature of globalization and what it would do to consumer markets. When I ventured to suggest that it might not be a walkover for them, my boss, a partner of the firm newly arrived from Europe, said, 'People (consumers) don't know what they don't know until they see it.' We would argue, among other things, about his belief that modern super retailers from the West would destroy the local kirana stores by 2000, and when I persisted that the outcome in India may be different because road infrastructure was average, car penetration poor, consumer diversity at odds with retail profitability and the kirana's relationship with customers very deep, he would ask, 'Why do you Indians think you are different? Does water flow uphill in India? Do you wear your noses in your ears?'

Since then, a lot of water has indeed flown under the India bridge, and even if it has not flown uphill, it has left debris of lessons in its wake. Cut to fifteen years later. What almost got me sacked then—saying India is different—and got me sent off on a grand tour of immersion in developed markets to broaden my limited Indian exposure to the world, has now become received wisdom.

Today, it is de rigueur for the same consulting temples to put out encyclicals that say, 'India is different; transplanting global strategies doesn't work.' In March 2012, an article by McKinsey titled 'How multinationals can win in India', written by three people from the India office, said unequivocally, albeit a bit too politely,

> Companies should avoid simply imposing global business models and practices on the local market. Over the past 20 years, multinational companies have made considerable inroads into the Indian market. But many have failed to realise their potential; some have succeeded only in niches and not achieved large-scale market leadership while others haven't maximized economies of scale or tapped into the country's breadth of talent.

Nor have they tapped into breadth of market opportunity. Rather gratifyingly for me, that article went on to say, 'For multinationals, the key to reaching the next level will be learning to do business the Indian way, rather than simply imposing global business models and practices on the local market.'[1]

In early 2011, an article also appeared in Harvard Business Review titled 'New Business Models in Emerging Markets' that said,

> But if the opportunity is huge so are the obstacles to seizing it . . . we believe they've struggled not because they can't

create viable offerings but because they get their business
models wrong . . . Many multinationals simply import their
domestic models into emerging markets . . . they may tinker
around the edges, lowering prices . . . but their fundamental
profit formulas and operating model remains unchanged,
consigning companies to selling largely in the highest income
tier, which in most emerging markets isn't big enough to
generate sufficient returns.[2]

Bain adds to this chorus, saying that to win in India, companies
must make 'bold long-term commitments to India', 'tailor their
offerings to suit the needs of Indian consumers', and 'leverage
global scale . . . but adapt locally to win'.[3]

We have a saying in India that unless water flows through a
conch shell, it is not deemed to be holy water, so now that the
high priests of management consulting have spoken, it is official.

This 'trickle up' of the idea that India is different has taken
a good ten years after Jim O'Neill of Goldman Sachs debuted
the BRICS report that said that, in future, the world's largest
economies would not be the world's richest economies, which
is the most fundamental reason why transplanting global business
models will not work. Global business models have been created
for markets that are large economies of relatively few high-
income people, and business economics that work there do not
work in large economies comprising lots of modest-income
people.

But Are Companies Listening?

What has been the progress in thought and action on the other
side of the fence—the main actors, not the drama critics?

For a start, there have been many more visits from global boards and global executive committees of the Fortune 100– 500 companies (and I have addressed several, because I am the shoulder from which local management fires the gun of 'please look at India differently, one "global" size doesn't fit us'. I have no career to lose and don't mind the frequency with which I get dismissed or politely listened to and then ignored). The bad news is that, for many, it is an all-too-brief visit comprising a five-star hotel stay in a big metro, maybe a visit to distant suburbs to 'get a feel of small-town India' and a lot of PowerPoint in a conference room. All of this leaves no space for exploring shifts in thought, driven by engaging with the contradictions and confusing things they see.

There have been many more MNCs who have deputed groups of mid-level 'high-potential managers' or 'young/future leaders' to embark on study tours of India, accompanied, in many cases, by an Ivy League business school professor as coach. Having addressed several such groups as well, I note that they 'get' the message that existing global templates may not work in India, but they are not at the level at which they can make a difference to the mindset and practices of the corporation.

On the plus side, the aggressive questioning of the 1990s and early 2000s from global boards and executive committees on why we need India when we have China is a thing of the past. That we need both is the accepted norm. That is indeed a huge win for India, and as global companies feel an increasing need to 'de-risk' China, more investments into India are being announced. Not all of the investment is for domestic market development but is typically for the combination of domestic market development and setting up global hubs of manufacturing, global R&D, data centres and back-office data services.

On the minus side, there is still a lot of resistance to three core ideas of what winning in India requires:

(i) Margins need to be reduced and volumes grown so that the total profit can grow. As a global CFO of a very successful global MNC observed, relaxing margin gates and allowing the business to have a low margin–high volume profile increases the overall risk of the business. The idea of different margin metrics for governing different countries has been what we in India would call slaughtering a much-worshipped 'holy cow', to be done at your own peril of bad karma.

(ii) New innovation (leveraging capabilities within the global organization) has to be done for the Indian market to unlock its potential, despite an available armory of global offerings; there is no other way to provide consumer-acceptable performance at consumer-affordable prices and a profit for the company.

(iii) The number of business lines launched simultaneously in India and price-performance points within each business line need to be large to unlock the India opportunity. As the CEO of one MNC said when this was recommended to him, 'Why do we need a Rolls-Royce approach to market segmentation and business lines for a market this small?' Why should Disney or Netflix invest in launching in so many Indian languages when the consumer segments delivering the required margin are so small? Because that is the difficult demand structure of the market, and without the effort, the addressable market will be even smaller.

The plus side is that more MNCs are looking at a 'one India' organization in India and departing from matrix structures of business line reporting which makes it hard to bring scale or explore innovations that fall between the cracks of business lines. The Indian managing director of a Dutch multinational conglomerate in the health technology business once said that he wanted to influence the 'strategy development policy' for the Indian company. I wondered what this meant, and he said he had to first detach India from the APAC (Asia Pacific) region so that it would become a standalone focus region. Then he could start the negotiation for a made-for-India strategy. PepsiCo, after almost two decades of being in India, elevated India to a 'region' status in 2008 with both the food and beverage businesses in it.

An increasing number of MNCs are structuring their presence in India as a composite of three opportunity or benefit streams, with varying weightages—the benefit of the domestic (new) market, the benefit of having a global hub for back-office work to increase efficiency and decrease cost and the many benefits that distributed R&D centres and other centres of excellence bring, as well as the benefit of having access to a high talent pool to export to other parts of the world. It is said that one of India's most successful exports has been middle-management talent, many of whom head large and prestigious global organizations. However, research talent in global R&D centres in India complains about not being entrusted with higher-quality high-end global work and, at the same time, not having enough freedom to fashion a research agenda that is relevant to India but does not fit global priorities.

The interesting question in today's day and age of a multipolar world is what the definition of a singular 'global' actually is.

Taking Stock of MNC Journeys in India, 1991-2023: A Selection of Stories from the Field

Even as recently as December 2022, an article in the *Economic Times* titled 'What makes some MNCs exit India' says, 'Though India is touted to be one of the fastest growing economies in the world in the next decade, many multinational companies have struggled to tap into the enormous potential of a nation with more than 1.3 billion people.' The report cites Holcim, Ford, Cairn, and Metro AG as examples of big companies that have shut shop in India or downsized their operations in the last decade. The article says the 'common reasons' were 'stiff local competition, an increase in losses, business models not aligning with the parent's global model, changing global market priorities', among others. Amazon, for example, has invested $5.5 billion in ten years, and its marketplace arm reported a loss of $800 million in 2019.

Even as Ford exited India in July 2022, the Volkswagen global chief of passenger cars said, 'There is more to come for us to play stronger in India.'[4]

Whirlpool, in India for thirty years, closed 2022 with a sales turnover close to $750 million, which is not a very great performance relative to the market opportunity of an under-penetrated consumer base thirsting for more durables. On the other hand, LG, in India since 1997, had a turnover double that of Whirlpool's at $1.6 billion in 2022. Both make home appliances in India, and LG also has a third of India's large TV market.

Samsung, another Korean home appliances and smartphone maker, entered India at the same time as LG in 1997. It has a

15 per cent share of the Indian smartphone market and is almost seven times larger than LG in revenue at $10.3 billion in FY 2022

Rishikesha T. Krishnan, author of *From Jugaad to Systematic Innovation* and professor at IIM Bangalore, observes in an article titled 'What does it take for MNCs to succeed in India?' that 'many multinationals have struggled to get it right in India. These include big names like Fiat and Electrolux and a host of Japanese companies including Sony and Panasonic. In contrast, Korean companies have been more successful, even though sometimes they entered [India] ten years later than their rivals from other countries.'[5] He observes, based on his research, that Korean companies made a strong commitment to the Indian market even before they entered and have been sensitive to the market by launching products more appropriate for India. He gives examples of how Hyundai changed its usual emerging market entry vehicle from Accent to Santro when it realized that Indians were looking for an alternative to Maruti Suzuki's market-maker, the Maruti 800. Another example he gives is of Korean appliance-makers, who were the first to provide a washing machine that resumed washing from the same point at which a power outage made it stop.

I remember, when LG refrigerators were launched, small-sized refrigerators with frost-free technology were a novelty. The market norm at the time was that smaller refrigerators were direct-cool and cheap while frost-free refrigerators came in a larger size and were more expensive. As a result, more affluent small nuclear families were forced to buy larger refrigerators if they wanted better performance! LG refrigerators also were designed with smaller freezers and larger vegetable trays to mirror consumer usage patterns. Unlike Sony, they delivered their technological superiority not just to the top-of-the-line, super-premium products, but also offered feature-rich and more affordable product ranges to a larger consumer base. They understood the long tail of India's income distribution and set up remote area offices in semi-urban markets. A colour TV priced just above black-and-white TVs for such markets was a part of the 'made for India' offering.

Maruti 800, Maruti Suzuki's initial and flagship offering for India, was another example of 'give them distinctly better benefits with as low a price as possible'. They did not launch with a model available elsewhere at dollar pricing converted to rupees. Launched in 1983 at Rs 47,500 with no air conditioning (less than half the cost of other cars like Ambassadors), and Rs 70,000 with air conditioning, Maruti 800 claimed fuel efficiency of 29 km per litre. Head and shoulders above existing offerings, it was a new-generation car that India had not seen before—packed with modern features, sleek design and low on maintenance, it quickly captured the imagination of upper-middle class Indians and became a status symbol and symbol of a new India. Maruti's revenue in 2023 is $14 billion.

Mercedes-Benz, at the other end of the spectrum, did the opposite. It launched with a smaller and older petrol model, the E-Class. The company admitted to making a mistake in not recognizing the segment of luxury car buyers who could have been anywhere-in-the-world consumers and would not settle for old models. An article in the *Business Standard* in early 2013[6] explained how:

> even as it introduced [the model that it did in India], new models of the [same E-Class] were ready to roll out from plants in Germany. As a result, affluent and prospective

Mercedes buyers in India, conversant with international trends, probably felt that they were being given hand-me-downs. Imported cars, two years old, were selling at about half the price of an Indian-made Mercedes, on top of that.

India leapfrogs. And while Volkswagen is seeing the future as 'when Europe goes predominantly electric after 2033, our ops in India have to play a prominent role to supply to regions not moving as far (towards electrification)', Tesla has announced investments in India to roll out an electric car at Rs 20 lakh for the Indian market in the near future.[7] (This price point is above the popular segment of Rs 5–10 lakh, which has 50–60 per cent of cars sold, and half the price of the high-end range of Toyota Camry or some of the Skoda and Volkswagen models).

The thing with the evolution of markets is that they don't follow a beaten track as MNCs often assume they will. Microsoft and Intel kept watching out for the desktop boom in India, while India leapfrogged to the mobile. After thirty years in India, Microsoft in 2021 had revenues of just about $1 billion.

3M, in India since 1998, has a revenue today of less than half a billion dollars. With its formidable innovation and R&D and range of businesses, it could have done much more in terms of products innovated for India. In my book *A Never-Before World*, I have some more commentary on 3M. It is a phenomenal company, in India since 1930, but with a turnover today of $1.1 billion. I remember thinking when I saw tea pickers in tea gardens leaving their babies in nearby hammocks that they have a great need for baby monitors (where the unit is placed in the child's bed and the receiver is with the mother). The Philips product, however, is priced at almost Rs 15,000 in India, and a cheaper version has not been made. Similarly, the battery-operated shavers at Rs 4000 are too expensive for where the need and volume really lie—with lower-income consumers, the liftman and office peon in Mumbai who need to wake up at the crack of dawn and commute two hours on a local train to get to work on time and do not have running water at home to shave conveniently.

Nestlé, in India since 1961, is a business that is very local in taste and preference. It an Indian MD after many decades in 2015. It has smartly built an India-centric portfolio within the boundaries of its parent business but has a turnover of $2.1 billion (small for a giant company), most of which has come in the last decade. Between 2002 and 2022, Nestlé's revenue has grown eight times. Maggi Noodles, launched in the 1980s, has been a great focus area for the company and has had endless work done on it in terms of product and positioning to make it a product created for India. Today, it is an iconic brand that is found in small-town street markets, where it is cooked by vendors using their own improvised recipes, as well as in upper-class metro homes. It is the comfort food of Indian millennials and the generations after them. It has innovated constantly for ingredients and flavours that work best for India, set up out-of-home consumption points and has consumers who co-create recipes with it across all regions and income levels.

Kellogg's, on the other hand, came to India in 1994 and has been determinedly crusading to 'educate' Indians to change and become 'global' in their breakfast habits. Who can say no to eating in the healthy international way, with convenience to boot? The Indian consumer did say 'thank you but no thank you', and Kellogg's has struggled in the market since then to build its India breakfast cereal business. In 2022, it had a revenue in India of about $170 million and a net profit of about $13 million. A WhatsApp meme doing the rounds says it all in terms of what finally happened in 2023. 'Kellogg's came to India challenging that they will change the breakfast habits of all Indians . . . 10 years later, this is what happened . . . Cut to pack shots of newly launched Kellogg's Upma (semolina-based savoury traditional Indian breakfast), ready to cook'. It is a three-minute ready-to-cook product called 'nutty upma'. Nestlé did a low-key launch of upma and poha (beaten rice savoury) around the same time, prepared just like noodles in a cup—add hot water, and it is ready to eat in five minutes. For rigid American and Swiss multinationals, this is quite a leap forward into 'localization'.

Since 2010, PepsiCo, under Indra Nooyi's stewardship, has had India develop Indian snacks for the local market and also use some of that knowledge in other markets. Kurkure and Nimbooz are some examples of this.

Colgate Palmolive has been in India since 1937 and has a revenue of Rs 5 billion or $649 million. An interview in March 2023 with the MD and CEO of Colgate Palmolive was all about how 'in rural India, only about 45 per cent of consumers "brush their teeth."'[8] (Question: If you rephrase the question as How many Indians *clean* their teeth, do you get a new answer and a new strategic insight?). She also bemoaned the fact that only 20 per cent of urban Indians brush their teeth twice a day. She said, 'Once we get consumers adopting the right oral care habits, there is a significant opportunity to boost volumes, and on top of that layer [premium products like] electric toothbrushes and toothpaste.'

The good news is that while Colgate Palmolive waits around for India to be ready for the Colgate version of oral care, unlike several MNCs, it is not saying, 'I will address the electric toothbrush and premium (value-added?) toothpaste market first and wait till more Indians qualify to become customers and afford these.' The bad news is that if this is the result of being in the market for almost a hundred years, then clearly there is something more or different that the market requires. On one occasion, I had suggested (quite out of turn and unasked, I might add) that since Indians are washing out their mouth and gargling all the time (and spitting on the roadsides as well), maybe a range of mouthwashes with medicinal properties would be in order? But then, that was not the Colgate way, and 'New York' (as Colgate India referred to the global head office) would never approve.

Honeywell, in India for thirty years, has a turnover of under half a billion dollars, while Siemens India is under $2 billion in revenue despite a long time here.

Coca-Cola, despite aggression and cumulative losses for a long time, is at Rs 45 billion turnover in 2022–23 ($562 million) and a profit of Rs 7 billion ($90 million), while the investments from 1993, when they re-entered India, till 2012 and committed from 2012–20 was $7 billion.[9]

Walmart has had an interesting journey of adaptation to India, pushed by laws that prohibit foreign participation in multi-brand retailing except as a 51 per cent owner and complying with a set of conditions relating to investments, local sourcing etc. On the other hand, 100 per cent foreign direct investment (ownership) is permitted in the wholesale business with fewer constraints, some of them being a required quantum of investment, and a minimum size of towns (one million and above).

Walmart entered India with a joint venture (JV) in 2006 with an Indian partner that would have enabled it to do both wholesale business and retail multi-brand business as well under franchise agreements with its partner. However, the JV broke up by the end of 2012 and cost Walmart $334 million, including losses of $234 million, to buy out its partner.

Walmart's then-CEO Scott Price said in 2012, 'I don't see how any foreign retailer can comply [with the FDI rules governing investment]', but also said Walmart was committed to India.[10] It continued with the now wholly owned wholesale cash and carry business (called Best Price), but with slower expansion than what one would expect from a truly committed Walmart, suggesting a strategic posture of 'build selectively and slowly and wait for the laws to change'. The opportunity for a modern value-added wholesaler in India was at that time (and still is) large, with 19 million small retail outlets, over 90 per cent of which are 500 sq. ft or less. While the law stipulates that the customers of Walmart should be retailers who are registered or licensed to operate, this would not have impacted the potential opportunity (small rural shops could have been aggregated under a semi-wholesaler who was licensed and helped to redistribute). Yet by 2020, Walmart's cash and carry business had only twenty-eight physical outlets operating and a mere 1.5 million members in nine of India's twenty-six major states.

In 2012, Amazon launched its e-commerce marketplace in India, as allowed by law to be a technology platform that facilitates customer–supplier interface. In 2018, Walmart leapfrogged into the e-world in India as well, at the same time it did the same in the developed world.

It invested in an eleven-year-old e-commerce marketplace called Flipkart (Indian promoters, Indian talent) and acquired a 77 per cent stake in it for $16 billion and an additional investment of $2 billion. As the *Financial Times* reported in a 2018 article titled 'Walmart renews bet on India', this move came after ten years of struggle to gain traction in the country! The article observes that 'nonetheless, the fact Walmart has hung on and is again committing itself to the Indian market shows how much promise the world's fastest-growing major economy continues to hold for some of the largest companies, even those that have suffered there before.'[11]

The suffering continues in terms of losses. In 2020, Flipkart acquired 100 per cent of Walmart's cash and carry company and Amazon also launched its own B2B business, making them both e-wholesalers.

As of 2022, Flipkart achieved a turnover of Rs 61,836 crore across both its businesses but with losses of Rs 7800 crore. The online marketplace achieved a turnover of Rs 10,660 crore but losses of Rs 4,339 crore, while the wholesale business accounted for the rest. Its marketplace business is a little over half of Amazon's, with about 18 per cent more losses. The consumer of course is the primary beneficiary in this fight for the market between the two giants.

Unlike some of the earlier MNCs, including so-called 'modern trade' majors who spent large amounts of money and incurred losses in order to browbeat a market into accepting a product with little customer-perceived value advantage, these losses are a play for dominance while delighting the customer with a stray customer-perceived value advantage.

IKEA entered India in 2018, very selectively geographically targeting six cities, three of which have physical stores. Even its online footprint is a conservative seven cities. It is clearly targeting India's upper-class, highly urban young households. In 2022, its revenue was Rs 1,076 crores and losses Rs 903 crore. While its merchandise and retailing format is very differentiated and price points very affordable for upper-income Indians, the distances and inconveniences in India's large cities with terrible infrastructure are a value detractor. The do–it–for–me culture is not a value-adder for Consumer India either.

IKEA's cautious and limited online footprint is a bit of a mystery though, because India's delivery infrastructure is very strong and used extensively by other household e-commerce and large consumer durables companies, even for large items to be delivered to remote corners of the country. In any case, IKEA does not offer installation and assembly facilities, unlike local furniture companies like Wakefit and Pepperfry. It could lead the Indian market with e-commerce and have physical stores as a selective strategy, given the size of a typical IKEA store anywhere in the world. Perhaps all this is a head office diktat—global strategy rules are that IKEA does not lead online.

IKEA has, however, announced plans to augment the mega-sized stores that they have with smaller-format stores that also serve to buttress the online presence as a planning, visualizing and advisory space for online orders. So perhaps round two for IKEA India will be to lead with a curated combination of online and small offline stores, seizing the room there is for more aggressive expansion.

Large private banks in India are also reshaping their legacy branch network to focus on small-size customer acquisition and advisory centres since most transactions are executed online either through a bank manager doing it for the customer or the customer doing it directly.

Levels were too low to sustain the scale at which they built theme parks around the world. The fact is that India's infrastructure, geography and income levels may never support the transplanting of global theme parks in the foreseeable future. However, the fact also is that if the future of Disney lies in staying relevant (and present to begin with) to future generations of the world, then being in India is essential. Perhaps Disney could have experimented with 'bite-sized' (for Disney, but large for Indians who have not seen theme parks before) parks in ten locations dotted all over India. These theme parks could have a hybrid model of low physical investment and a virtual reality-type tech augmentation and be designed for a high volume of visitors with low spending each, which is in line with India's income structure. After all, the idea is to create the happiest or most magical space on earth, and Indian children are ready for that. Obviously, the franchising strategy of properties so created would have to be customized too.

That aside, Disney's journey in India since 2003 (when it terminated its Indian partnership and restarted as a wholly owned subsidiary) has been a series of flip-flops both in commitment and strategy. One would have expected more commitment and longer-term thinking for a market that holds a large proportion of the world's future children. China had infrastructure enabling theme parks but no free television, while India had the reverse. If the goal was to build a Disney generation in a country that speaks twenty languages at least, where there is no similar competitor, where there is a very rich culture of storytelling that goes back thousands of years, where the society is child-obsessed, then much more expansiveness, both strategically and in terms of execution, was surely warranted? In 2023, Bob Iger, global CEO of The Walt Disney Company, expressed his disappointment with the company's performance in India, especially as Disney+ Hotstar lost IPL cricket rights to a domestic company (though it did capture the rights for the Cricket World Cup some months later). Of course, this is a fair distance away from Disney's erstwhile focus on families and children and a still-open opportunity to cash in on its core market.

On the children and family front, Disney Channel launched in December 2004 in India, airing Disney original shows that did not resonate with its audience too much. It took till 2011 to do a local adaptation of a live-action international series, 2012 to produce a second one, 2016 to scrap this line of content, 2015–17 to tie up with Bollywood for local movies and change their mind on it and 2016 to experiment with Japanese animation content and acquire a local channel along the way. By 2020, after a global acquisition, Disney+ Hotstar became the home for Disney content, which was getting lost in the prolific Star general entertainment local languages content. Still, Disney+ Hotstar is also slower in original regional content than its rivals Netflix and Amazon Prime Video—India is now a hotly contested entertainment market. Also, in keeping with 'global strategy' (and 'global' and Western age demographics that are not the same as Indian age demographics), the share of children's content in Disney+ Hotstar has fallen in India too. As a result, Indian children between the ages of 0–14, who represent 26 per cent of India's 1.4 billion population, remain underserved and have missed out on growing up with Disney.

Perhaps treating India as a special focus market, an autonomous, standalone strategy-developing and executing entity, and leveraging Disney's rich historical competence in the children and family entertainment arena would have been a win-win for both Disney and India.

How Have New-economy MNCs Fared in India?

From 2005 onwards, the new-economy companies started entering India. As was discussed in the chapter on digital India,

Google, WhatsApp, YouTube and Facebook have captured India and been embraced by Consumer India who perceive life-improving benefits in what they have on offer.

Other iconic new-economy companies like Uber, Airbnb and Netflix have entered India with aggression—their stories are a bit different from the old-economy companies because they are young and evolving and therefore less hidebound about what their winning formula is and what is not their way of playing. They also had an easier and faster ramp-up because the digital tech platform is easily transplantable across markets, India's tech infrastructure is much better than its physical infrastructure, and their business model is asset-light. They also have more local competition because the entry barriers of tech platforms and business models are less formidable to surmount. Venture funding to support losses is the critical ingredient, and this is more welcome across country barriers.

In fact, even before new-economy companies came to India, there were clones who set up shop. The next chapter will discuss some of the 'made in India' new-economy businesses, many of which are actually solving problems and creating businesses that are unique to India, combining tech ability, local knowledge and customer intimacy.

Netflix launched in India in 2016. In 2022, Netflix CEO Reed Hastings said in an interview that the company was 'frustrated' that it could not get to its targeted subscriber base in India. According to a BBC news report in January 2022, in February 2018, he told a global business summit in Delhi that the next 100 million customers would come from India because of cheap internet. It achieved an estimated 5.5 million paying subscribers as opposed to 46 million for Disney+ Hotstar and 19 million for Amazon Prime Video (which are much cheaper).[12]

Since then, Netflix has slashed prices by 20–60 per cent, depending on the subscription plan (mobile only, single device became cheaper by 60 per cent) and that has raised volume by 30 per cent. Consumer India is, however, spoilt for choice, with seventy-five streaming services in various language combinations and a lot of free-to-air television channels (600 at the last count). Pricing for TV is regulated and, in 2023, 100 free-to-air TV channels can be accessed for as little as a Rs 130 connection fee. Even remote India has operators with satellite dishes and very low pricing.

Netflix maintains that despite the distance from its targeted subscriber base, India is still the fastest-growing market in the world in 2022. Analysts and Netflix have commented about how much Indians like local content and, like Disney learnt, partnering with Bollywood isn't easy. In fact, Spotify is quoted to say in an Ernst and Young report that 83 per cent of time is spent on local content in India as opposed to 49 per cent of time elsewhere.[13] Analysts also say that Netflix uses its 'international playbook' to develop content for the Indian market and so is still seen to be foreign. Further, it caters to a 'class market' audience, while its aspiration is for the mass market. Password sharing is also very rampant in India, but cracking down on it is going to be harder here with 'mobile only' basic plans and so on.

Uber and its local rival Ola are neck to neck in India in Uber's core product market of cars. Uber services 123 Indian cities, Ola 160. Ola also pioneered three-wheeler autorickshaws and bikes, and showed Uber the route to a broader user base. In India, Uber also offers autorickshaws in several cities. Competition is stiff for both customers and suppliers.

Given the low penetration of cars in India, mostly owned by rich households, Uber's model in India could not use part-time drivers with own cars, in a peer-to-peer sharing model, as is the case in other parts of the world. Uber drivers in India are full-time drivers—this is their day job. Therefore, they are either employed by taxi companies already who are listing their cars on Uber or are 'own account workers' who need to buy a car first in order to become Uber drivers. The statistics on car penetration that we saw in the section on market structure show that with the really low penetration of cars and purchasing power being restricted to the top end, there are no under-utilized cars or any cars for that matter in potential drivers' homes. This requires Uber to tie up with banks and financial institutions—as their India blog a year after launch in India said, 'We have partnered with top lending companies and created vehicle financing schemes with low down payments, superior finance rates and faster turnaround time exclusive to Uber . . . as well as worked out exclusive discounts with [car manufacturers].'[14]

This also means that drivers have to pay EMIs on their loans out of their earnings and are not sweating an owned asset. As Bloomberg columnist Andy Mukherjee pointed out, 'It's not a capital-light business in India.'[15] It also added to business model fragility during economic slowdowns, as was seen in 2018 and 2019, when NPAs of banks on account of Uber loans increased sharply. If capital and resilience are key to Uber's success in India, the model needs strengthening. Banks pull back loans when driver incomes fall, and several banks have discovered a prudence after the first flush of lending on this account and lightened credit norms. Ola, Uber's local competitor, also suffers from similar issues.

Airbnb lists India as its focus market. As in the case of Netflix, to get to the number of users targeted globally India is an essential market, aside from the opportunity itself on a standalone basis. Airbnb claimed 70,000 listings in India in 2021 and very steep growth trajectories. It also said in its official business briefings that its hosts made Rs 100 crore in 2022 and that it has captured a lot of India's outbound traffic.

Airbnb exemplifies the strategic fluidity of new-economy companies. It has stayed true to its core model of being a platform connecting hosts and guests and giving freedom of pricing to the hosts. It has retained its focus on 'alternate experiences and customizability', but in 2019, it also invested in OYO Hotels and Homes, a local competitor with a different business model and value proposition. It also lists OYO on its own platform.

OYO is an aggregator of budget hotels, guest houses, homes and, to a lesser extent, workspaces and wedding venues. It franchises the OYO brand to the properties and works towards setting standards and taking responsibility for implementing the same. It also caters to and designs specific propositions for wider segments than Airbnb, such as longer-duration stays, workspaces, wedding venues and so on. OYO is cheaper than Airbnb on average and caters to a larger and less affluent mass market that wants standardization and basic assurance of the brand in order to manage its travel well, rather than seeking experiences. Where Airbnb takes 3 per cent of the booking value from hosts and 6–12 per cent from guests, OYO takes 22 per cent of the booking value from hotel owners. OYO has global ambitions, has grown rapidly internationally and retreated ignominiously as well, but it proves to be an interesting competitor, complementary and a potential acquisition for Airbnb, which is also looking at the hotel space globally with its acquisition of Hotel Tonight.

That is another observed difference between old- and new-economy MNCs in their approach to India. Both have aspirations and estimates of what revenue they may get that are not necessarily grounded in the reality of the strategy they deploy. However, new-economy companies are writing their own 'mother' playbook even as they are entering and expanding in India. Hence there is far more amenability to go after differentiated opportunities that present themselves in the Indian market. Also, because top-line (user base more than revenue) expansion leading to valuation is still the name of the game for many, the competition for capital across markets based on the return on invested capital does not seem to be there.

Amazon is perhaps the most amazing of new-economy entrants that has captured the imagination of mass and class India. While Netflix and Uber have still ended up catering to a particularly more Westernized cultural class, Amazon has pierced the mass and class market and has used its formidable competence to build a marketplace of incredible range and variety. It even has varieties of packaged cow dung available on it, and almost every kind of local food grain, herbal health supplement, gym mat, wet grinder and anything at all, supports the incredibly varied lifestyles of India which lives over four centuries, as is often said.

Its 'made for India' curation of 'everything you and your grandmother ever wished for or thought about' has earned it a brand relationship of great dependence and authority, as the WhatsApp joke doing the rounds so brilliantly captured: A husband asks his wife to buy X, Y, Z for the house, and each time she says, 'Why don't you ask Amma *Jaan* (beloved mother in Hindi/Urdu) for it.' In frustration, he says, 'What's my mother got to do with this?' It turns out that she is referring to Amazon (Amma Jaan). Apart from English, the Amazon app supports seven Indian languages, though even before the app was launched in languages, people who didn't know how to read and write English were navigating it by scrolling through pictures or asking someone to help them. The low prices, the no-questions–asked easy returns and the ability to deliver almost anything almost anywhere in India made it the big box retailer of choice for the country. With Amazon, India has leapfrogged from physical marketplaces to e-marketplaces by skipping the Walmart era altogether. Of course, there still exists the hyper-personalized small physical shop (I have an electronics products supplier, but now I show him Amazon prices, which he perforce matches or else he loses my custom), and there are hyper-local gofers using apps, who will get me groceries in no time at all from the nearest physical store—all coexisting and adding to customer delight.

Key Takeaways: What Holds Global MNCs Back on Their India Journey? Why?

I have often asked myself why global companies, which are so successful and have super-bright management, fail to 'get' what it takes to win in India and to get it done, given their phenomenal execution capabilities. In a hallmark article in *Harvard Business Review* as early as 2003, called 'The End of Corporate Imperialism', C.K. Prahalad and his co-author Kenneth Lieberthal called out the MNC mindset and presciently said that even as MNCs will change emerging markets forever, the reverse will also be true.[16] Many of the examples we have just discussed underscore this. They said in the article that 'large Western companies . . . [entering] emerging markets . . . were guided by a narrow and often arrogant perspective [that] countries like India and China [offer] vast agglomerations of would-be consumers hungry for modern goods and services'.

The article says that the first wave of market entrants has an 'imperial mindset' because it assumes that the emerging markets are 'new markets for their old products'.

Subsequent waves of MNC entrants have continued to struggle. If 'imperialism' was the first mindset, it gave way to the second mindset of 'gosh this is really underdeveloped; we will come back when the market is ready for us'. As India's GDP steadily climbed up the world rankings, demonstrated resilience and was clearly here to stay as a much-needed alternative to China, India increasingly got put on the front burner for Western MNCs and of course the Korean, Chinese and Japanese companies too (as has been discussed earlier in this chapter).

The word 'frustration' is cropping up more often nowadays when 'head office' business leaders talk of the progress of their India business relative to expectations. In absolute terms though, they also laud the growth that they see relative to other parts of the developed world.

The frustration is partly due to the legal, government and infrastructure environments and the general ease of doing business in India. Partly, it is with the stubborn market and consumers that refuse to evolve the way they 'should' and 'ought to' along the beaten path that many markets before them have. This frustration is of the same kind that is heard when geopolitics is discussed. Why doesn't China follow the 'rule' that with increasing economic prosperity should come increased liberalism? Why doesn't India follow the 'rule' that there is a pecking order in the world and it must align on global issues? India's foreign minister said in a 2019 speech at the Atlantic Council, 'It is what I would call a Goldilocks era of our relationship, which is: the West didn't want India to get too weak, it didn't want India to get too strong. So, it . . . tried to stir the Indian porridge just right.'[17] Stirring the porridge of the India strategy 'just right' to not rock the global business principles of a successful company but yet exploit the full power of India's large and growing GDP is the source of a lot of frustration. It also frustrates CEOs and business leaders on this side of the table, in the subsidiaries' offices. I often hear the refrain 'This needs to be done, we agree, but HO will never allow it' or 'We need to work on HO to get a buy-in and it will be a long haul'.

The broad headings of the sources of frustration can be described as follows:

(i) *World view:* A wholly incorrect dominant logic that the evolution path of all markets in the world is the same. Clearly, India today is not China ten years ago or Europe twenty years ago. The ugly duckling, modest-income, cell phone-and internet-enabled Indian market will not become the familiar beautiful swan of a yesteryear Western developed nation today or in the future. This is all the more so for an increasingly nation-proud Indian consumer growing up at a time when the idea of globalization itself is rapidly changing. The world views on what is best practice for global businesses have also changed considerably, acknowledging the multipolar worlds and new theories from academic high priests on how global businesses need to move from one-size-fits-all to more granular multi-country strategies. Pankaj Ghemawat, a professor at IESE Business School in Barcelona, who is an acknowledged thought leader on global business, has developed a framework called CAGE, which is a way of understanding differences between countries that should inform international business strategy. The framework identifies cultural, administrative, geographic and economic differences. When applied to markets and consumers, India's cultural (including business and consumer culture) and economic differences (including the demography of people and firms that drive the economy) need more than minor adjustments to global strategy.

Once the dominant logic of global companies changes from the 'uniform pattern of evolution, hence all markets will travel down a beaten track that other markets have trod before them', it is easy to see that a modest-income, modestly educated, highly aspirational, digitally empowered consumer base existing with poor infrastructure and mostly 'own account' employment will need different things and will process value differently from other consumer bases. Add to it a hugely entrepreneurial small supplier environment, and the nature of the market changes even more starkly from others. With this new world view, it will also be easy to see why the earlier generation of India strategies have not worked and are quite suicidal, especially for the India of today. They reduced prices by reducing performance, decreased functionality and styling, and offered old or obsolete products with no local adaptation in order to meet global margin norms.

The new way of squaring the circle of price-performance-profit has to be through innovation in terms of business model and R&D and ruthless process (digitally driven) efficiency. What C.K. Prahalad called 'the NEXT practice'.

(ii) *Governance:* This has been discussed earlier in the chapter in the context of matrix organization structures, margin gates and time frames over which returns are mandated but bear repetition. In the new-age model of the global firm should different markets/economy types have different evaluation metrics by which they are governed? To me, the obvious answer is 'yes'. However, global CFOs say that moving to a low margin-high volume type of business in any one market causes huge issues in managing risk. But then, finding ways to manage different genres of risk and de-risk the risk basket is the CFO's job and is what investment banks have been doing forever.

There is also a lot of concern about the governance of the global brand. Perhaps the new rising focus on the 'purpose' of a business (hence the core values of its brand) should make it easier for global brand custodians to allow freedom of brand communication under a common umbrella of 'purpose'.

'To entertain, inform and inspire people around the globe through the power of unparalleled storytelling' or 'making lives better by powering a more prosperous world' do have different communication pegs in different parts of the world.

(iii) *Prisoners of past success formulae:* A mindset of a singular or templated evolution pattern down a beaten track leads companies to want to follow the same formulae of success that have been followed in the past. So, no mobile-first, e-commerce after; no different order of execution of business lines, healthcare first, home care later; no simultaneous launches of old and new horizon businesses for auto or power companies and so on.

The point is that the race that they ran when they became champions is not the same race that they will run again to succeed in India. The nature of the race and the competitors may be totally different. I have written about this at length in my previous book, *A Never-Before World*.

(iv) *Value arrogance:* The Western business academic community did everyone a disservice in the early days when China's strategy was hotly discussed, by coining the word 'good-enough products'. It suggested two segments—(global) great products and (local) make-do products that are less effective. This has led to a lot of value arrogance and blinkered and segmented perspectives on what competition exists.

R. Kannan, the founder of Vortex Engineering, which launched India's first ATM built for rural areas, the Gramateller (solar-powered and low-cost) asks the question, 'What is an eighty-year-old rural lady's definition of quality in an ATM? The "world-class" quality definition of six pieces of currency per second doesn't apply at all to her low-value transactions, but a biometric interface adds a lot of value for an illiterate person who says, "I cannot keep my money safe with just four numbers."'

Salesforce.com has a 'good-enough' Indian competitor Bizom, which is becoming the preferred SaaS (software as a service) offering for large Indian consumer packaged goods companies. Built for the large unorganized retail ecosystem that such companies deal with, it can deploy in weeks and does not need months of customization and attendant costs. MyGate, an Indian visitor management and security system, would also probably be characterized as a 'good-enough' solution to Honeywell and similar big global offerings in the same space of security management for large condominiums and buildings. But it has gained traction, designed as it is for the environments of an Indian building society/housing community with the mobile as a basis and dealing with barely educated security staff with high turnover, all kinds of household help who are often a multiple of family members coming and going and a maze of resident WhatsApp groups resolving community issues. They also offer applications to help resident welfare associations manage their expenses, billing and so on.

Here's the irony: 'Good-enough' solutions have failed in India not because the offering was inferior or feature-light or performed worse in getting the job done. On the contrary, they are often better on all these counts. They fail because the small companies who have created them run out of money in the process of scaling or diversifying revenue streams too early in order to survive and then collapse because they are unable to manage the many irons they have in the fire.

The large global companies have deep pockets and resilience but not the appropriate solution or the mindset to use their capabilities to design 'good-enough' solutions that work better for the environment they are to be deployed in. Seems like a marriage made in heaven, but Barkis is not willin'!

(v) *Conflicting strategic intents*: 'Strategy for this market' or 'market for this strategy'? One very dominant theme in how Western MNCs think about India (or indeed about any emerging market) is that it should serve as an extension market for the treasure trove of products, services, R&D and business models that they already have. On the one hand, the readymade fruits of their hundreds, even thousands of years of experience around the world are assets that must be sweated. On the other hand, there is a desire to exploit/ gain as much as possible now and in the future from a large new market. In the case of India, which needs a 'made for India' strategy that leverages what is available but does more than transplant. I call this the conflict between 'market for this strategy' and 'strategy for this market'. CEOs are told to deliver results commensurate with the full size of the market using templated 'global' strategies and implementation modules that are capable of addressing only a part of it. Interestingly, global companies are ready to incur losses in 'educating' customers in new markets on appreciating their offerings better (read 'spend to pummel the market into submission') but not willing to spend even a part of the same amount of money in developing solutions that really work for the market.

In many ways, this goes back to the question of how country subsidiaries are governed.

(vi) *The stressful economic challenge that India poses:* Unlocking the potential of the Indian market requires the mass market of India, not just the top of the income and sophistication pyramid, to be captured.

As has been discussed so often so far, the challenge of unlocking the mass market in India is to create *customer-acceptable* products and services for demanding customers at *customer-affordable* prices (or total cost of ownership) for modest-income consumers. Further, these have to be delivered at a *profit to the company*.

Creating a customer-perceived value advantage over the competition is further complicated by the range of 'good enough' options available in the market and the consumers' ability to curate a portfolio that delivers the highest value.

Overcoming the stressful economic challenge posed by mass markets requires companies to set a 'challenge price' and define the performance criteria of the 'job to be done' to customer satisfaction. The challenge price is the price at which the (benefit–cost) value perceived by customers is better than the value they perceive from the competition (competition could even be the non-usership of any solution and living with the problem). Obviously, 'challenge cost' is the variable to be controlled by the company since the other two challenges are set by the customer! This requires breakthroughs in R&D to slash costs (not easy and takes time) and/or business model innovation. It involves exploring a full spectrum of variables to balance.

In the next chapter, some examples will be given of how this was done using 'frugal' innovation and how, at last, new-economy business models are able to crack open the mass market and scale—the new way of designing 'made for India' businesses.

Strategic Choices for India

- Transplant? 'Glocalize'? Translate?

Chart 1 summarizes the spectrum of strategic choices available

Orientation	Market what is globally already available	Localize global model where possible	Create locally for a new market
Dominant Logic	• Extension market to exploit (transplant)	• Extension market with localization (Glocalise)	• Build customized to win in India (Translate)
Where to play—customers	• Customers who can afford and need global products **Top of the pyramid, X% of GDP**	• Choose most affordable product range and business lines from global repository • Bigger slice of top of the pyramid	• Customers who have the need and whose challenge price-performance I can innovate for **all of the pyramid**
Where to play—business lines/products/use cases	• Standard global practice and sequence of introduction		• As per local need and need gap opportunity and global competencies and resources
Growth drivers	• Increases in income and sophistication of India's business and consumers	• Increases in customer income and sophistication • Ability for local manufacture and optimizing supply chain	• Innovation capability • Investment appetite • Time horizon
Margin control	• Unit level gross margin fixed at global norm	• Unit level gross margin fixed at global norm	• Unit level gross margin flexible, pooled gross margin fixed
How to play	• Global value proposition, branding proposition and go to market model	• Global value proposition • May have second brand • Localise go to market model	• Whatever is appropriate

Each of the options clearly has different pain and gain pay-offs and different shapes of investments and returns over time. Strong India office business leaders who have credibility with the head office manage to negotiate at least some 'create for India' play.

- Is there a benefit to the popular idea of establishing a premium beachhead and waiting for the market to evolve?

Many MNCs operate with this idea: 'Let us serve the top of the income pyramid that can afford us and wants superior performance. The middle of the income pyramid will be served by those who deliver inferior performance at a lower price. We will wait till consumer incomes increase (i.e., "our" benefit appreciating high-income market grows over time).'

The flaw in this logic is that like time and the tide, mass markets also do not stand still and wait for anyone. There are a growing number of rapidly upgrading local options that are offering the required performance at far lower costs. The mass market is getting better served with time. In fact, it is getting transformed and not sitting in the dark ages and waiting to be able to afford a 'global' supply. This should cause a sense of urgency in addressing the mass market today.

- Business rules of the global corporations that constrain India's strategy and need to be re-examined:
  - ⇒ Margin and volume mix to meet profit goals.
  - ⇒ Speed of payback vs investing for a longer time horizon to build a strong growth engine that can ride on India's long-term growth with the power of compounding.
  - ⇒ Strategic complexity allowable for current market size.
  - ⇒ Metrics for different markets—do they all have to be the same.

7

Unlocking India's Mass Market Opportunity: Frugal Innovation and New-Economy Digitally Led Models Show the Way

India's mass markets have been very hard to unlock because of the challenge of satisfying customers *and* being profitable, and they have been ignored by most large companies. Over the years, several constituencies in India have addressed this challenge, and a treasure trove of experience and market-tested pilot models abound. Add to this the 'frugal innovation' capability, the new digital capability and new-economy models now available to lead the way, and the mass market in India is on the verge of receiving the fruits of a huge supply revolution that will be a win-win for suppliers and customers.

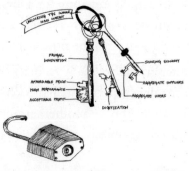

Designing Businesses for India's Mass Market: India's Journey So Far

Households in the middle and bottom of Consumer India's income pyramid have over half of the income and expenditure of Indian households, and yet they have been underserved by most large companies, more so by MNCs with their imported business models. This segment abounds with underserved 'blue ocean' market opportunities and lots of unaddressed pain points. However, the challenge this segment has always posed is how to deliver consumer-acceptable performance (that 'gets the job done' properly or better than available options) at consumer-affordable prices (or cost of usage) and yet make a profit from doing so.

A lot has been argued in earlier chapters of this book on why serving the mass market (the middle- and lower-income groups of the income pyramid or the belly of the income diamond, depending on how you choose to draw it) is so important to companies wanting to secure their future in India. To briefly reiterate the point—it is large; it is steadily growing its incomes and consumption and will likely double both in a decade; it is hugely desirous of consuming and is exposed to what is available to richer folks to make their lives better; it is underserved and abounds with unaddressed pain points and opportunities for value addition if only the formula to serve it profitably can be found.

When a value-adder to their life at the right price-performance is offered, this segment embraces it like no other. The use of UPI for digital payments has been the most recent example of this. WhatsApp is another example; HUL's Fair & Lovely, though not politically correct nowadays, is another example of what can happen when solutions to the fundamental needs of Indian men and women are appropriately met. Two-wheelers (delivering over 100 km/litre and mileage–power balanced) and Chinese goods (never-available-before, highly affordable solutions) are examples of penetration that can happen in modest-income segments when consumer-perceived value is delivered.

Figure 1 summarizes the stressful economic challenge posed by India's mass markets of balancing performance, pricing and profit. This has required getting investments and operating costs to the lowest possible level without compromising performance (getting the job done well) which has been the focus of a lot of constituencies in India. Scientists, big businesses, small entrepreneurs, innovator communities, social businesses and incubators have all been working on this in various fields, striving to be cost warriors through better process design, product design and more insightful 'spec' design of the job to be done.

While many of the attempts at achieving this have not grown into blockbuster businesses, they are an invaluable treasure trove of market-tested, pilot-scale innovations as well as valuable lessons which large companies can leverage. More importantly, the culture of going to war on cost and being able to achieve performance at the lowest possible cost is deeply ingrained in India and is a badge of honour and pride. Not too long ago, the word 'jugaad' used for innovation in and from India had the meaning of 'cheap, cheerful, gets the job done in a makeshift way'. It now carries a far more evolved meaning. Google it today, and the responses are 'a flexible approach to problem-solving that uses limited resources in an innovative way', and 'non-conventional', 'frugal innovation', 'hack' or 'workaround'. So too has the meaning of 'frugal innovation' evolved. Originally it referred to creating products or services that are very simple and made from locally available materials by those who could not access the 'real thing'. Now it is widely used in India (and in this chapter) to mean innovation to reduce costs and complexity by stripping out the components that add cost but do not add to customer-perceived value; or to getting the required output or outcome at the lowest cost. The Indian orientation has changed from 'doing the best one can with limited resources' to 'proactively limiting resources and yet getting the job done perfectly'. It is also seen as a war on waste.

Noted economics analyst Shankkar Aiyar writes about Indian cost competitiveness in an article titled 'Domino Effect of Scale and Indian Cost Competitiveness'[1]: 'Indian brands are pioneers of price engineering through product design. After all, it was the Cuddalore-based CavinKare, a blend of the Tamil phrase for beauty and care, which introduced the world to the scale of opportunity embedded in sachet marketing of products with Chik shampoo' (more in this chapter). India's value-for-money warriors have enabled scaling low-cost production for the Ikeas and Walmarts, he goes on to write. He refers to the cost reduction through 'localization'—in terms of supply chain and manufacturing—that many MNCs have done in order to offer cheaper than dollar prices of imports. Samsung and Apple have exported smartphones worth over $10 billion (made in India, outsourced manufacturing), he points out.

Frugal cost engineering is visible in complex scientific projects—the budget for Chandrayaan 3 (the moon mission of India's space research organization ISRO) was a fourth of Tom Cruise's latest movie. India's space research organization has attracted world attention for frugal engineering in its Mars mission as well. An article in BBC titled 'Why India's Mars mission is so cheap – and thrilling' says that India's mission Mangalyaan cost $74 million,[2] while the NASA Maven mission cost $671 million. Mangalyaan used a smaller payload, which gave them less scientific investigation capability, the article says, quoting experts, but India has been smart at complementing what others are doing and will still address the biggest questions on the Red Planet. A principal scientist at the NASA Maven mission has been extensively quoted in the media on how, in the absence of powerful rockets, Mangalyaan used a series of small rockets burning at different stages to get to its destination. 'I thought it was a very clever way to do it,' he is quoted as having said. Jugaad to get to Mars![3] This has definitely captured India's imagination and strengthened the jugaad gene.

The digital revolution in the world (and sweeping through India), the new-economy business models coming out of America of platforms of many kinds and the sharing economy have provided the tools, the examples and the inspiration to give this mindset a quantum boost.

A new breed of Indian start-ups has mushroomed, not just from large towns and those educated in prestigious college campuses, but from the length and breadth of the country and people with varying levels of education. As of October 2023, India had 111 unicorns and a significant increase in funding, with both local and global investors. Of course, this world waxes and wanes, and some unicorns have lost status in subsequent rounds of funding. However, taken together as a group, they have amply demonstrated what the new low-cost–high-performance scalable model is to crack India's mass market and add disproportionate value to consumers at the lowest cost ever in the Indian business experience. There will be a lot more in this space that will dazzle the consumers and make them even more spoilt than they have been so far.

Figure 1 also depicts the two ways in which the challenge posed by the Indian mass market has been cracked—by old economy business models using frugal innovation to deliver all three, price performance and profit, and my new-economy business models using new thinking made possible by the power of digital to do the same This chapter describes, by way of illustration and not comprehensive chronicling, some examples of how Indian companies over the past twenty-five years have thought about and crafted low-cost high customer-value 'made for India' businesses targeted at modest-income consumers and micro businesses. The examples have been selected to capture the diversity of thought, problem-solving approaches and solution spaces.

The first of the two sections that follow gives examples from the old-economy world where frugal innovation was the key and the second section is from the new, emerging world of the new-economy, digitally-led business models.

Figure 1: Cracking the challenge posed by the mass market

Mass market business challenge

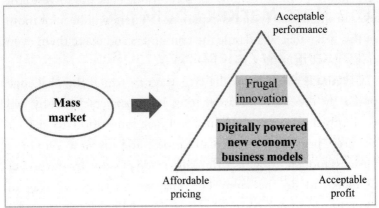

Section I: Old Economy Models Using Frugal Innovation to Crack the Mass Market Challenge

Providing 24/7 Electricity for Basic Needs to Households

During summers, when power usage is much more than power availability, many towns in India experience 'power cuts' or 'load shedding', which obviously cause a lot of stress in people's day-to-day functioning and efficiency. The higher-income households can afford solutions like solar panels, inverters or even generators. Lower-income settlements in small towns and more so in the villages are the sufferers. The make-do solution of the smart small entrepreneur that has been celebrated in many articles is for him to invest in a solar panel and retail 'pay as you use' power to people, i.e. get them to bring all their gadgets in the daytime, especially torchlights (made in China, of course), and get them charged and ready for the night in case of power outages. Several small entrepreneur models like this are dotted all over the country—another example is selling filtered water to those who can't afford a water filter. Interestingly, this is the old version of the sharing economy that was popular in India before the so-called sharing economy/new-economy arrived in the world. However, clearly, this is a solution that, while being better than darkness, still leaves much to be desired.

An IIT Madras team led by Prof. Ashok Jhunjhunwala observed that for as much as 12–14 hours, the electricity supply grid had a voltage that was too low for the AC to be able to power anything in the home. Hence, while the grid could provide low voltage 'brown-outs', it was effectively a blackout. Could the low voltage be put to use to give enough power to households to have a few basic amenities?

The team defined the 'job to be done'[4] as providing 24/7 'minimum required power' at a consumer-affordable cost. They defined the minimum required power as enough to sustain two 18-watt LED bulbs, two fans of 30 watts, a cell charger or one fan and one 24" LED/LCD television. The team innovated a low-cost DC power solution for individual households that could give households power even when receiving lower voltage from the grid.

Building a solution that utilized 'brown-outs' required (i) a power utility sub-station to supply 'brown out' power instead of shutting down fully; (ii) DC appliances that run on low power (LED lights, brushless DC motor fans and modern power electronics already exist); (iii) two power lines in the house—an AC circuit for normal power supply and a DC circuit for low power supply; (iv) something that can sense low voltage 'brown-outs' and switch the household to the DC circuit or sense voltage return and switch it back to the AC circuit. The product innovation was a small gadget that senses voltage changes, cuts off one line and feeds the other.

This was a win-win solution for all—the power utility which could now do better than it was doing with the full power/blackout paradigm and the households that could get power through the day with very little capex. The module in 2015 was estimated to cost $20 at peak scale of production, the DC line for the home was configured to 100 watts and 48 volts so that the same wiring as the AC line could be used for convenience. The cost of the wiring would be $11 or so (at 2015 prices). LED lights are already a feature in most low-income homes because of low power consumption and the ability to function across more voltage fluctuations. Modern power electronics like cell phones require DC in any case. Manufacturers are happy to do low-power DC gadgets because of the cost and problems of power converters.

Examples from Healthcare

Aravind Eye Hospital is a case study from India that is globally acknowledged as a pioneering example of low-cost excellence in healthcare. It uses an innovative process model that enables it to successfully perform large volumes of cataract surgeries at a fraction of the cost prevailing anywhere in the world. This has been described in two articles in *Harvard Business Review* in 2010: 'What Poor Countries Can Teach Rich Ones About Health Care'[5] and 'Could an Indian Hospital Help the US Cut Health Care Costs?'.[6]

Narayana Health, also using focus and a standardized, well-controlled process, has been aptly described as the 'Henry Ford of Cardiac Surgeries' by the *Times of India*[7] (and is also a case study at Harvard Business School among others). The Southwest Airlines model of healthcare has become familiar to the Indians even as it coexists with top-of-the-line models that are as good as the best of the West.

Product-led models are also in plenty. Forus Health defines the job to be done as getting people to the doctor on time to avoid preventable blindness due to delays in getting treatment. The cost of doctor consultations is high also because of the investment in multiple devices the doctor has to keep because devices are problem-specific and not general purpose. They innovated a pre-screening imaging device that can screen for many conditions, is non-invasive, compact and portable, can be operated by a minimally trained person and works on any Windows PC/laptop. It captures high-resolution images of the eye through a quick focus mechanism that speeds up examination time and has integrated record management facilities and telemedicine modules. All this makes it easy to use for mass rapid screening programmes. It is now available for sale in the US, Canada and Europe. The branded device 3 Nethra is priced at around Rs 6,00,000.

Telemedicine is now well-established and popular the world over. In India, it is extensively used to connect remote areas to hospitals in big cities and save costs and the lives of those who do not have the money to travel to a hospital (and also incur costs of the attendant family who need to travel with them and stay at the location of the hospital).

The same also applies to remote diagnostics. Mobile diagnostic vans that go from village to village are a popular phenomenon with NGOs and hospitals for their social outreach programmes and will become a more popular telemedicine model soon because scale in rural areas comes from consumers paying small amounts each and a wider geographic footprint. It is only possible if services are taken to consumers rather than the other way around (which adds to consumers' costs and deters them from seeking medical help before it is too late). It is also true that working with not very well-educated paramedical staff and technicians is only possible if the equipment is sophisticated and demands minimum user adjustments/interventions. For the job to be done properly, the equipment must be in good condition when it gets to the user over bumpy, dusty, potholed roads and paths. Most equipment is usually very delicate and frequently gets spoilt. In this situation, L. Kannan of Vortex Engineering, which is also the creator of the low-cost ATM widely deployed in rural India, identified the solution to be a better design of the mobile van, making it better able to protect its contents, rather than engage with the tall task of trying to make the equipment sturdier! He designed vans that have special suspensions and also typically come custom-designed such that they open out into different rooms for a better flow of patients.

Kannan also looked at the textile business, which is a large employer in India, and has small producers at every stage except the stage of conversion of cotton to yarn. He then applied his mind to the problem of how small producers (cotton growers and weavers) could get a larger share of the value chain of what is a large and growing end-user market for apparel in India. He observed that the stage of conversion from cotton to yarn was the exclusive preserve of large companies with very large capacities, and the largest cost in the value chain was the stage of compressing cotton into bales and transporting them to large-scale spinning mills; yet every other stage before and after had a very large share of small producers. He started asking whether there was any reason beyond history for this, whether it could be downscaled and where economies of scale could lie if the model was disaggregated. The answer is a patented technology called Microspin, where an entire end-to-end small unit can be installed in 3,000 sq. ft, at a fraction of the cost.[8]

'While a conventional spinning mill would have a capacity of 25,000 spindles, a Microspin mill would have a capacity of 500 or fewer spindles. The machine cost and cost of training etc. would put it at a total cost of Rs 1 crore. Add dyeing and weaving units to make it an end-to-end mill, and the total cost would be Rs 5 crores as against Rs 100 crores of a conventional mill'[9]; the smaller scale also works because players in the non-yarn part of the chain are also small-scale. A single Microspin unit according to them can support 80 hectares of cotton farm, twelve looms, and twenty sewing machines. India, incidentally, has an estimated 6 million cotton farmers with an average farm size of 1.5 hectares against the average size of a US cotton farm, which is a little over 200 hectares. India contributes to 26 per cent of global cotton production and is the largest producer of cotton in the world. Started in 2011, this is yet another example of the amazing library of market-tested innovations that are yet to become mainstream, going beyond pilot projects here and there.

This solution also enables innovation in yarn and premium fabrics like *malkha*, found in high-end designer collections, which is a product of this company.

The poster child of India's frugal engineering was a small car from Tata Motors, Tata Nano, the most affordable car in the world. While it was praised by the global auto industry for engineering excellence that it showed the world, it was not a market success because it didn't get the 'customer acceptability' leg right, especially in communication and positioning.

Nirma, the soaps and detergents manufacturer (among other things the group does) pioneered the low-cost business model in the late 1980s and gave Unilever in India (Hindustan Lever then, now Hindustan Unilever, HUL) a run for its money. It made them develop a whole new business model from manufacturing to go-to-market and create a whole new business unit and christen it 'popular detergents'. (Side story: they originally called the business unit 'low-cost business' and their original business unit was called 'mainstream business'. Young managers wanting to protect their career paths preferred working in the 'mainstream' business! So, it was re-christened 'popular detergents' and later the 'popular foods' business came into being).

The famous shampoo sachets, pioneered by Cavin Kare, made mainstream and scaled hugely by HUL, was another uniquely Indian solution that delivered affordable pricing per use for customers who used shampoo occasionally. It gave them the 'real thing', not a weak, lower-performing version of it, and was per millilitre more profitable for the company as well because of the price point they could pitch it at (perceived value price delta that they could get).

The 'prepaid' model of telecom usage, both voice and data, which accounts for 88 per cent of subscribers, is another example of 'sachetization'. As a result, the consumer wins and the company also wins by not incurring any credit cost or billing costs.

The purpose of this section was to provide a peek into Indian innovation and to give a glimpse of an alternate business logic that innovators in India are developing (as opposed to the old quest to be world-class, defined just like anyone else in the world). In *We Are Like That Only*, I directed readers to the work of Prof. Anil Gupta's Honey Bee network of grassroots innovators, who are regular folk, often barely educated, who innovate for themselves because nobody is doing it for them. It has also been observed that Indian consumers innovate better than companies, illustrating it with a set of examples starting with the 'missed call', the ingenious way by which telecom company revenues are curtailed but networks used. A missed call from your chauffeur says, 'I am here', a missed call from your courier says I have delivered your parcel and so on!

The next section gives examples again by way of illustrations, not complete chronicling, of India's new-economy, digitally-led business models, which are the future of India's market, and the low-cost, high-performance formula for companies to serve the mass market of India better and profit from it.

Section II: New-Economy Business Models Using the Power of Digital to Crack the Mass Market Challenge

An analysis of 102 unicorns and 124 'sunicorns' (those which may become unicorns in the next four years) shows that there is a very wide range of arenas addressed by Indian start-ups including fintech, health tech, edtech, marketplaces of all kinds, sharing services, lots of B2C e-commerce, social media and entertainment, agritech, logistics and distribution and a range of B2C services. This section describes the ones I have found more interesting because they have managed to tap the 'blue ocean' uncontested spaces that were unaddressed latent needs; or because they have managed to bring together existing fragments of an industry and harness them into a proper and complete ecosystem, benefiting everybody (rather than build every element anew). There are, of course, this being India, many smart copycats of new-economy businesses from America, tailored to India—OYO and Ola, inspired by (and gone beyond) Airbnb and Uber respectively.

Core Business Model of Successful New-Economy Mass Market Players

Chart 1 summarizes the requirements on both sides of the table that have to be met for a successful mass-market business in India to really work.

Chart 1: Demand and Supply requirements to play in the mass market

Demand side	Supply side
Reduce price to what I can afford BUT retain performance above my acceptable threshold (to get my job done to my specs)	Keep margin above acceptable threshold levels (do not make risky margin x volume bets)
Enable occasional access to the real high value thing that I cannot afford, within my budget, whenever I need it	Enable 'sachet-izing' and efficient sharing of the high value 'real thing' item between multiple customers without margin sacrifice
I am small ticket and/or remote located. Fulfil my performance requirements with **NO** location or small ticket price penalty	Get unit margin positive when serving them. Meet revenue goals by cost effective geographic scaling to manage long tail

Meeting both demand and supply side requirements was nearly impossible to do at all and certainly not at scale in the old world that did not have digital capability and when new-economy thinking had not been invented and demonstrated in America.

But now, there are four levers, made possible by digital capability, that can crash operating costs and enable businesses to meet customer performance and price demands while still being profitable:

1. *Aggregating users*: In a market where a lot of people buy a little bit each that adds up to a lot, aggregating users can provide the increase in ticket size per 'user' (aggregated unit) to make costs work better. Several business models based on buying groups have come up, especially for the low-income mass market.

   This works for small businesses as well, and B2b2c models are getting popular (Big business serving small business and small consumers).

2. *Aggregating suppliers:* This is an asset-light new kind of business model that is common around the world. It is perfect for India, because of the profusion of small suppliers who already exist and can be aggregated to provide cost-effective supply. Execution is still hard when it comes to aggregating and disciplining them, but not as hellish as it would have been in the pre-digital era! Also, this explains the popularity of marketplaces and the many two-sided platforms that have become increasingly popular for matchmaking between buyers and sellers. Small buyers and suppliers make up the core of India's mass markets and good marketplaces, and two-sided platform owners provide reassurance to buyers that earlier only large brands could provide. Swiggy, the food delivery app, aggregates street food vendors, not just large restaurants, and gives mass market consumers the same convenience as its higher-income consumers without their having to go to big restaurants that they can't afford.

3. *Enabling sharing:* High-value durables like cars, designer clothes or tractors can now be seamlessly shared. Because of India's demand structure, rentals have always been a popular model. The previous section discussed the small entrepreneur who 'rented' or shared solar power from his solar panel to users. Various community use models have been created often by the local communities themselves. When television manufacturers were puzzled by the sudden increase in sales of large-screen TVs in early 2000, their investigation found that richer rural households were sharing their TVs with the community (for a fee of course). Now, with digital capability, the cost of execution of rental models has crashed, and efficiency both of asset utilization and availability on time to consumers has increased.

4. *Digitalizing processes:* This has perhaps been the biggest new development in India, enthusiastically embraced early on by all large companies who put a 'digital nervous system' into their business operations to crash costs and expand operating margins as well as meet regulatory requirements for inclusion of low-income consumers (especially in the case of banking and also telecom-related services,). With the spread of digital public utilities and with government services also going digital, small suppliers too, have started digitalizing processes aided by a whole ecosystem of IT services providers that help them with simple mobile-based software and services. Embedding 'digital' into all business processes has crashed costs and helped businesses achieve the table stakes needed to qualify to play in the mass market.

As was discussed in the section on behaviour, modest-income India loves the digital way of doing things—it saves time and money, is more accurate and provides status-blind service. Yet, the most difficult part of business operations to digitalize has been customer-facing processes and Indian businesses of all sizes and generations struggle with it though they are going up a steep learning curve. Understanding where such processes fail is critical. Quite often, the customer's preferred way is 'do it for me' and a digitally empowered human interface needs to be designed which is able to capture a lot of the cost savings that come from digital 'do it yourself' customer-facing processes. In most businesses that are doing this digital reengineering of customer-facing processes, there is a war between the high-tech digital folk and the high-touch frontline, customer-facing folk (especially those serving modest-income rural or urban consumers). At a non-banking financial company (NBFC) lending to mass-market rural customers, there was a big push to digitalize the process of collecting money from borrowers every month. The argument was that this would result in significant cost savings because it would enable getting rid of the large army of collection staff who visited customers every month to persuade them to pay their loan instalments; and if customers were not able to pay at that time because of the erratic and lumpy nature of rural income, to understand his future cash flows and agree on a payment schedule. Collection efficiency was also a business performance metric that the stock market analysts tracked for rural lenders. The customer-facing teams at the branch pushed back and said, quite rightly I think, that 'unless I visit the customer's house, I will not see that he has a new refrigerator and not know that he has come into money in recent times and that is critical information to make him pay up.' On the other hand, an insurance CEO digitalized customer-facing processes that stopped mis-selling altogether and saved a lot of risks (from complaints to the regulator who believed in caveat venditor if customers were sold products that were financially unsuitable for them). Sales agents from his company are equipped with a tablet with custom-built software, where the agent enters the customer's responses to a few questions relating to respondent profile and risk appetite and it throws up a set of suitable product options, outside of which the agent is not permitted to sell.

Business models that deploy these levers can break long-accepted compromises[10] ('it is what it is, there is no solution, let us live with it') that customers and businesses have had to make and that have held back the unlocking of India's mass market opportunity at scale.

Chart 2: Compromises that needed to be broken for mass markets to be cracked

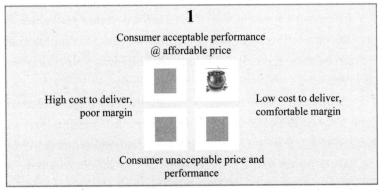

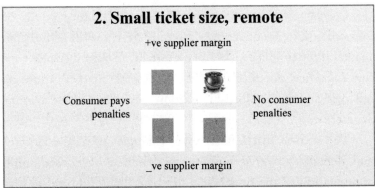

Chart 2 shows the three big compromises that existed and needed to be broken if India's mass markets were to be profitably served.

Compromise 1 to be broken: Customer-acceptable performance at customer-affordable prices cannot deliver a comfortable margin because the costs to deliver are too high. Something has to give.

Compromise 2 to be broken: Serving customers in remote areas who have small ticket sizes (i.e. spend very little per purchase or have very small balances in their bank accounts) requires either the customer to pay a price penalty or the supplier to have a negative margin.

Compromise 3 to be broken: High-priced luxury goods or consumer durables or services can only have a small addressable market if the supplier makes a comfortable margin (because very few customers can afford it). The addressable market cannot be enlarged and made affordable to more customers unless margins are sacrificed.

The section that follows gives examples of new-economy and digitally-powered business models that have used some combination of the four levers to break the compromises that exist in the market. As discussed earlier, these examples are to illustrate the new kind of thinking that will shape the future of India's consumer markets rather than to chronicle success stories.

Some Illustrations from Business Models of Unicorns and Sunicorns of How These Compromises Have Been Broken

ElasticRun: Value-Added Rural Market Distribution for Remote Rural

The business concept

Existing distribution systems for companies, especially FMCG companies, do not reach below a particular village size or town size. Distribution to micro retailers who service small customers in remote rural areas that lie beyond the existing distribution systems is done by the wholesale market. For the micro retailers, this spells uncertainty of supply, higher and unstable prices (leading to their own customers not trusting them) and higher effort and hence cost in ensuring procurement when there is demand.

The business concept of ElasticRun is to become a (digitally powered) value-added distributor to these underserved retailers by procuring directly from the company and extending all the benefits that even bigger retailers in larger locations get (low inventory, frequent replenishment, returns) price stability, company schemes, etc.). The benefit to the company is obvious.

They are aggregating a network of micro retailers in rural India and enabling consumer goods companies to reach further at a far lower cost than they could themselves. Through the same 'pipe', they are experimenting with offering banking services on behalf of banks as well.

Enablers of low price-high performance

Aggregating demand and digitalized processes are key features of this B2B model.

Aggregating demand from micro retailers in a predictable manner enables ElasticRun to buy cheaper and directly from companies and capture the wholesale margin (exactly as modern trade does).

This is a zero-capex model, and costs are almost totally variable.

The feature that is most out of the box for me is the most challenging and potentially high-cost logistics piece of collection and delivery to retailers. It is done here using an Uber model, i.e. build a network of 'feet on the street' (delivery people and maybe their two-wheelers) using the same principles as Uber. Since there is manpower in these areas that are not engaged full-time in productive work, this is a win-win for both the part-time employee and the company.

'Think by machine deliver by human' is the founder's credo for low-cost performance delivery.

DeHaat: Value-Added Wholesaler and Marketplace for Agricultural Inputs and Produce

The business concept

DeHaat provides small farmers (small ticket size, remote location consumers) with a one-stop shop from 'seeds to market access for their produce'. As is well-known, all the price penalties of small size and remote locations and low staying power apply to small farmers. They are typically served by small local retailers who have the same deficiencies as was described in the ElasticRun case study.

DeHaat leverages this existing network of micro retailers and strengthens and enables them to deliver a wider range of products more efficiently and earn more—a win-win for the customer and the micro retailers as well as the value-added wholesaler.

Through this 'pipe' of efficient micro retailers, it is looking at disseminating advisory services and perhaps later even offering software services for farm operations. Their value proposition to farmers is the ease of access and one-stop service for input purchases and output sales; the efficiency of the digital world is offered to all and there is also the human face (the micro retailer) for fostering trust and keeping costs low! Not engaging in battle with a local, well-entrenched ecosystem of retailers but co-opting them into the business is a win-win for all sides.

Enablers of low price-high performance

- Through aggregation of demand done at two levels—at the level of micro retailers and therefore at the level of small farmers that the retailers collectively serve. This aggregation helps DeHaat to get more large partners onto the platform (input companies, output buyers, facilitator services providers) and grow (and protect the ecosystem they create).
- A local network of small entrepreneurs (micro retailers) when supported with skills and knowledge and digital efficiency can bring a new energy to serving customers with a human interface, bring and manage people resources for the last mile and hold inventory.

- Digital processes are used wherever possible and sensible, to crash costs.
- Partnerships are built to expand the range of offers, using this platform.

Similar models like this exist. AgroStar, for example, has a business concept of being an end-to-end support platform for the small farmer. Their mix of offers includes tools and inputs and customized advisory on crop planning and rotation, soil nutrition etc. The 'watch out' for agricultural models which involve advisory services is that the farmer does not see much value addition in them and is not willing to pay for them. Either the services have to be far more advanced and customized or advisory services are to be thought of as free components that build customer stickiness for paid services. The AgroStar customer lead generation model is interesting—customers are asked to give them a missed call (to be followed up by the company). These models are all good examples of phygital business models.

Marketplaces Are the Future: Where Small Suppliers Meet Small Buyers with the Assurance and Services of a Large Platform

The marketplace model has captured India's imagination. India is leapfrogging from crowded large high-street physical stores and physical marketplaces full of small shops and small buyers to crowded large e-marketplaces full of small shops and small buyers. This has been easy because structurally nothing much has changed, so it is business as usual but on a larger scale, thanks to digital footprints being larger and not expensive. The suppliers and buyers also have digital savviness and prefer the benefits of a digital marketplace and small suppliers tell us that their children are unwilling to be in a business that requires them to sit in a physical shop in a crowded marketplace all day but are willing to stay in the business and build it via a digital marketplace!

Amazon has taught India what the highest operational standard of a marketplace is. As for knowing what support services the platform owner must offer, the same support services that physical marketplaces offer would work in the digital space too—painters hang around paint and hardware shops, transporters of all kinds are present, credit is extended and so on. Fully migrating these services onto e-marketplaces is probably yet to happen. India is seeing a lot of e-marketplaces getting built and will see a lot more in the future.

Some well-funded marketplaces are Zetwerk for industrial tools and machinery manufacturing, which attracts small vendors as much as the big ones. OfBusiness serves manufacturing and construction sectors which abounds with small businesses. They offer raw material procurement (deriving and offering, as all large modern retailers did, price advantages due to aggregation of demand) and credit services to help customers buy better, timely, and cheaper.

Infra.Market is also the online marketplace for procuring all sectors of the construction ecosystem, which includes not just materials but also heavy equipment rental etc.

Udaan is the poster child of Indian e-marketplaces, having become a unicorn early on. It is a B2B trading platform for buyers and sellers of 5,00,000 products at least. Goodbye tramping in and around chaotic physical markets—the small sellers and buyers can now live better and earn better! Square Yards is a property ecosystem marketplace. Financial marketplaces abound—PolicyBazaar for insurance of all kinds is one example. Their proposition to buyers? 'You get more than just financial safety. You also get our promise of simplifying complex insurance terms and conditions, quick stress-free claims, instant quotes from top insurers, best prices, unbiased advice, storage of policies online' and all large insurers on the platform.

India has always loved and hated traditional middlemen. They were the grease that made the chaotic wheels turn smoothly, brought knowledge, information, connections and access to the table, as well as credit and much more. Even though they are not transparent and are not seen to be totally trustworthy, they foster sticky relationships with their customers.

E-marketplaces are familiar in function and form to the middlemen—they are just more easily accessible, offer genuine choice (middlemen traditionally have monopoly territories and gentlemen's agreements between them) and have the potential to be more transparent and foster more trust.

This model is the one that India has already embraced, and it represents the future of competition.

Digital Gold: Micro Ticket Size Gold Transactions

Indian households are, collectively, the world's second-largest consumers of gold. Cultural and social reasons are aplenty, such that even the lowest-income family will try and buy a little bit of gold every few years. It is seen as the safest and most liquid asset class and, especially for women, the best source of financial security. The trouble has been that low-income consumers have never been able to buy micro quantities of gold, and even the little that they bought (a few grams minimum) came with the 'penalty pricing' that accompanies small-ticket purchases, as well as the inability to check the purity of what they were buying. They also cannot sell small quantities of gold because it is not worth the while of the traditional system to allow them to do so.

Several players, fintechs mostly, along with other lines of business as well, have enabled low-income consumers to safely buy and sell gold, even in very small units (and broken the second compromise discussed earlier, of retaining margins for the seller *and* not punishing the customer for small ticket sizes.)

PhonePe, Paytm and SafeGold are examples of this. Consumers can transact in amounts as low as Rs 5 (one gram of gold retails at close to Rs 6000 today).

Business concept

Buy, sell, and gift gold in very small quantities. The gold is safely delivered home or warehoused in a physical gold locker that you can digitally check. Therefore, households and women can safely save in very small quantities as and when they have surplus money and let it accumulate for use when needed.

Except for the physical handling of gold, all processes are digital.

Enablers of 'no small-ticket penalty' for either buyer or supplier

This model works because it aggregates a large number of small buyers cost-effectively using end-to-end digital processes and at scale, it can be buying and selling large amounts of gold and gaining from the scale economics of doing so. The price of gold to small buyers will be slightly more than the market price, but a fraction of what it would cost them to buy and sell on their own at traditional jewellers. Further, the gold is not in the form of jewellery, where solders etc. reduce the value of the gold weight and is impossible to accurately estimate, leading to rule-of-thumb discounts to the weight made by most jewellers. When needed it can be redeemed and exchanged (since gold is now hallmarked in India, there is no problem with establishing the genuineness of the gold when exchanging it at a jeweller's shop for ornaments).

There is also a very small gold storage fee charged to customers, but lower than the risk of loss when stored in their homes. Overall, the price to the customer is lower and benefits are higher than traditional channels of gold purchase and sale.

Micro Accident Insurance

Prime Minister Modi announced an accident insurance scheme for low-income Indians that all insurance companies were required to offer. It was a very small premium of Rs 20 per annum and coverage of Rs 2 lakh for full disability due to accidents and Rs 1 lakh for partial disability. This scheme was offered by an insurance company that had a very advanced digital process environment—and they completed all customer-facing processes via text messaging and had a fully automated back end.

They reported unprecedented 'walk-in' demand for the service and, on a fully loaded cost basis, they said it was profitable despite the small ticket size. Cost saving was on account of having no customer acquisition costs, the low cost of onboarding customers and a non-linear cost of scaling. I remember observing that this proves two things—one, the fallibility of the insurance business dictum 'insurance is never bought; it has to be sold', and two, that the prime minister has better consumer insight than the marketing department!

DealShare: Buying Groups for Small Customers and Regional and Local Small Brands

Business concept

DealShare enables low-income consumers to form buying groups and choose from over 1000 products listed.

The platform sources backwards and gets the best price for whatever the group wants to buy. It is targeted at small-town modest-income consumers, who are happy with locally sourced 'does the job' products that are not even listed on Amazon (and are cheaper).

This is a modern convenient system of an age-old practice in several Indian households—forming a buying group with neighbours and going to the distant wholesale fresh produce market where prices are low but minimum buying units high. Transport costs would be shared and price–quality optimized.

Enablers of low price-high performance

Demand is aggregated so that both the platform and the consumer groups get lower costs, reverse sourcing for everyday low prices, enable consumer sharing, screen and list very small local and regional suppliers who want to increase sales. And of course, all processes are highly digital.

Meesho: Drop shipping/Reseller Business

This model has gone through many changes, but the original business concept to me seemed like a winning idea, conceptually. Execution challenges are probably quite stark and, like Uber, all platforms where a gig-working battalion is crucial to the model, the sharing of revenue between the platform and them is always an issue.

Business concept

Conceptually, Meesho used to be the wholesaler for a range of large and diverse products which enabled resellers to sell under their own brand/label using social media networks they had or were good at building.

The platform handled all logistics and operations for the resellers, and they were encouraged to build their business. No explicit fees were charged but, presumably, a volume of business-linked discounts existed.

Enablers of low price-high performance

There were no end customer or reseller acquisition costs for the platform and no logistics or operations costs for the reseller because they were doing social commerce, using free or very low-cost social media as a means of demand generation. The platform received the benefits of demand aggregation and used digital processes to slash costs.

Rural Banking: Providing Universal Access to All Indians

India has managed to get near-universal delivery of basic banking services. Before the digitally-led new-economy model showed the way, bankers would complain about the 'cost-income ratios' of lower-income bank accounts—how the balances there did not justify the cost of transactions in that account, and how forced inclusion targets by the banking regulator were making them lose money.

The fixed cost of branches did not justify the demand at any location or catchment area, given rural India's geographic scatter. ATMs were also expensive (hence the innovation of solar ATMs discussed earlier). Yet the regulator had mandated going to unbanked rural areas as the condition for permission to set up new urban branches.

Today, the whole paradigm of a 'rural bank branch' has changed thanks to the creation of the institution of digitally powered banking correspondents. They are either a one-person roving branch or a fixed-location small shop and offer full banking services (including cash dispensing and collection, initial processing of 'paperwork' for applications, and selling third-party products as permitted by regulation).

The banking service works despite the very limited physical presence of the bank because of the digital capability that is brought to the banking correspondent. He or she can access the customer's bank account via a cell phone because all bank accounts are Aadhaar-linked, and all Aadhaar is linked to the person's biometrics. With a small biometric reader attached to the phone, banking correspondents can establish the identity of the customer and the authenticity of his bank account. The banking correspondent can also connect to the bank operations and perform most functions that a fully staffed bank branch could in the old days.

As the government has started sending social benefit cash transfers directly to the bank accounts of beneficiaries, the balances have increased (though people tend to withdraw most of it in cash); add digital payment penetration to this mix and the virtuous cycle of win–win for all is beginning.

Enablers of low price–high performance

The digitalization of processes has significantly crashed costs and eliminated large, wasted overheads of physical infrastructures and permanent employees. The whole KYC and verification/authentication processes are now digitally enabled. Fewer ATMs are required even as the geographic footprint of customers served expands (in the section on old economy innovations, we discussed the solar ATM. Today it is the human ATM of the banking correspondent that makes solar ATMs obsolete). Aadhaar Enabled Payment System (AEPS) enables this payment for amounts up to Rs 10,000 per transaction. It is operated by a public utility and is free of cost but doorstep payment fees will be charged to customers (this is again lower than what it would cost her to trek to a branch or an ATM).

Demand is aggregated because the branch (banking correspondent) moves and serves a larger catchment area at a very low cost, and supply is also aggregated with banks having multiple banking correspondents.

Social Media and Entertainment for Mass-Market Consumers

There are several other models of serving the mass market of which ShareChat is one—a 'below the nose' alternative to Facebook, Instagram and WhatsApp that targets low-income users who are mostly not comfortable with English and is designed for a small-town audience that needs its own platform.

Supporting fourteen languages with user-generated vernacular content, it has a whole host of features—anonymous chats, private messaging, TikTok-type user-generated video sharing etc. This platform says it wants to help individuals who are not very confident in the English world of global apps (with their token language enablement to form substantial connections—a local, low-income LinkedIn!) and stay entertained.

It goes a step further than the larger more established social media and teaches people to use it—what is a feed, why do you follow somebody, how do you create content etc. Revenue comes from ads, sponsored campaigns and payment transactions.

There are several regional OTT platforms with local content springing up. Readers will recall the discussion in the behaviour chapter on the increasing popularity of vernacular language content in India, including on large OTT platforms.

EdTech: High Demand but Delivery System Still Work in Progress

In child-centric India, given the incredible ever-growing hunger for better education to get children to progress in life, edtech is a very popular area for start-ups. The field can supplement school and college teaching and coach for the innumerable competitive exams that young people need to take. These models aim to offer much lower-priced coaching than physical models or single entrepreneur–teacher models. However, the jury is still out on learning outcomes; some edtech start-ups have added physical arms, and the realization that high investments in content and R&D are needed despite it being a digital model with cheaper delivery and reusability is still a dampener. Further, far greater quality assurance is needed by edtech platforms of teachers they get on the platform. This continues to be a huge area of demand, especially with less advantaged students who need to make up for the poor-quality teaching in the schools and colleges that they attend. However, the experience in this sector has been troubled on a variety of counts. It may go hyperlocal and phygital or the winning model may be a large ecosystem with several smaller ecosystems in it.

Postscript

Many of these start-ups have yet to find their path to profitability, especially as they scramble to scale for valuation at speeds of customer acquisition that are not matched by their ability to service them.

However, they do represent a major breakthrough in unlocking India's mass markets comprising middle- and bottom-of-the-pyramid households of Consumer India. And Consumer India is very pleased with it all and venture funding is betting heavily on it.

The New Face of Supply and Competition in India

- Digitally powered marketplaces and platforms, specialized by sector and region, are here to proliferate.
- More small suppliers will thrive and be born with easy access to markets via platforms and marketplaces.
- Hyper-local and niche small businesses can now be serious competition to the big players—the low investment needed to go digital enables them to do so easily and effectively and they can focus on customer intimacy, experience and service in their little niches.
- Full-service solution platforms can make it hard for monoliners who want to play alone unless they seriously up the benefits of the expertise of some kind that can make them differentiated and with more customer-perceived value.
- Phygital models will work better than pure-play digital.
- Consumer India will become an even more spoilt, demanding creature than it was before!

Postface

The 'People View' of India's Economy

For over two decades now, my professional interests have centred around bringing the 'people view' into business strategy and public policy. One strand of this has been my work in the area I describe as 'customer-based business strategy', on which my consulting practice and my teaching are based. The other strand, which is the territory of this book, is what I call the 'people view' or the 'macro-consumer and macro-citizen' view of India; I think of it as a sort of sibling to the macroeconomic view.

My macro-consumer journey of over two decades began with my engaging in many ways with the work of NCAER (National Council of Applied Economic Research), where economists worked alongside statistical survey folks and pioneered a longitudinal data set on how Indians earn, spend and save. It then took me to People Research on India's Consumer Economy (PRICE), a not-for-profit research centre that I co-founded around 2012 to continue the work NCAER had stopped doing in this field. Thus, the ICE 360 data set was born and three rounds of it were done in 2014, 2016 and 2021. In 2023, I decided to move on from PRICE and look at a wider research agenda and bring the 'people view' lens to a broader range of issues.

Some examples of the new scope of work: A 'macro consumer and macro citizen' study of young India is a work in progress, being done by a team of young anthropologists. Analytics to find non-ad hoc ways of socio-economic segmentation of Consumer India is in progress with a team of data scientists using ICE 360 and other public and proprietary databases. Also work in progress is an attempt at thought leadership around the important questions of 'what defines a genuine middle class, how large is it in India and how to expand it?' It builds on a research paper by Mastercard Center for Inclusive Growth titled 'From Middle India to the Middle Class of India' that was published about a decade ago in collaboration with the author.

There are lots of other issues where the people view, obtained in a way to represent all Indians, can add insight to macroeconomic data, as well as the dimensions of 'how and why'. I hope that there will be a way for me to engage with them going forward. A few examples: The people view of the savings rate of households—who (which demographic, where) is saving differently and why, would add value to the macro number; A much deeper understanding from the people view of how India exactly earns—deeper, sharper occupation categories, its predictability, time use etc.—will enable us to understand labour productivity better and in a more granular fashion, as well as understand and predict consumption swings better; People-level data on understanding the nature of informality in terms of access to networks, tools for improving productivity and upskilling opportunities would be a useful input to policy.

I am hopeful that over time there will be many more sources of interesting and useful data and conclusions centred around the 'people view' of the economy and society for business and policymakers to factor into their decision-making and solution designing.

Acknowledgements

I am often asked 'How do you go about writing your books, what's your process?'

And the truthful answer is that my books are written chaotically, in fits and starts, with numerous partial drafts written in no particular order. I muddle through the book, agonizing and to-ing and fro-ing on the structure, the grammar, the data presentation and lots else. The only way all this ends up in something resembling a coherent book is because of a highly engaged band of supporters and cheerleaders who have helped me with the heavy lifting and offered ideas, constructive criticism and help with problem-solving.

A heartfelt thank you to:

MRUC and Kantar for allowing me access to data and analysis of IRS and World Panel respectively.

Magic 9 Analytics, Mahesha Sahoo and Praveen Tripathi, for analysis of ICE 360 survey data.

Rajesh Shukla for being an integral part of my PRICE years.

Karunya Gunavathi for designing all the charts and tables—you exemplify the new young India that I write about. Sitting in Tenkasi, deep in Tamil Nadu, you digitally offer state-of-the-art graphic design support to customers far away.

Avishi Surekha, for your creativity and enthusiasm, your probing questions and the hours you spent, despite your many other commitments, in illustrating the chapter titles.

The Penguin Random House India team for all their work in making this book happen. In particular, Radhika Marwah, my ever-calm editor, who forgave me for my endless WhatsApp messages as she steered the book forward, and Shadab and Gunjan for giving me the amazing book cover that I love so much.

Sudhir Arora for being such a great sounding board and for patiently engaging with me at every stage of this book, at all odd hours, for the better part of a year.

Lucy, without whose help and hard work my efforts would come to nought. Thank you for always being there for me in all my life's major endeavours.

Never least though often acknowledged last, are the two amazing women in my life, my daughter Aparna and my mother. They inspire me, energize me and make me give my best with their 'come on, you can do it'. Aparna, time and again, you have pinpointed where this book was going wrong and offered exactly the right solutions. The mantle of 'my insightful in-house consultant' that was once dad's is now yours. If he were here today, he would have been both delighted and relieved!

Notes

Chapter 1: God Is in the Detail

1   'India is likely to be the world's fastest-growing big economy this year', *Economist*, 12 May 2022, https://www.economist.com/briefing/2022/05/14/india-is-likely-to-be-the-worlds-fastest-growing-big-economy-this-year.

2   More details in Rama Bijapurkar, *A Never-Before World: Tracking the Evolution of Consumer India* (New Delhi, Penguin Books India, 2013).

3   Vidhi Doshi, 'Gurgaon: what life is like in the Indian city built by private companies', *Guardian*, 4 July 2016, https://www.theguardian.com/sustainable-business/2016/jul/04/gurgaon-life-city-built-private-companies-india-intel-google.

4   'Smart pickup in good jobs', *Business Standard*, 28 November 2022, https://www.business-standard.com/article/opinion/on-sentiments-smart-pickup-in-good-jobs-122112801008_1.html; 3400 listed companies reported 9.3 million employment in 2020-21 and 3315 listed companies (a slightly smaller set) reported 10.1 million employment. Therefore, one million plus jobs had been added.

5   'Domestic consumption is our biggest strength, says chief economic adviser Anantha Nageswaran', *Economic Times*, 7 October 2022, https://economictimes.indiatimes.com/news/economy/policy/domestic-consumption-is-our-biggest-strength-says-chief-economic-adviser-anantha-nageswaran/articleshow/94690107.cms.

6   Churchill in a speech to London's Constitutional Club in 1931.

7   Lee Kuan Yew, as quoted by Farid Zakaria in 'The rediscovery of India', McKinsey.com, 1 November 2013.

Chapter 2: A Framework for Understanding Drivers and Shapers of India's Consumption

1   Rama Bijapurkar, *A Never-Before World: Tracking the Evolution of Consumer India* (New Delhi, Penguin Books India, 2013), Chapter 1, pp. 14–15.

Chapter 3: Making Sense of the Structure Story

1   Rakesh Kochar, 'How We Did This', *The Pandemic Stalls Growth in the Global Middle Class, Pushes Poverty Up Sharply*, PEW Research, 18 March 2021, https://www.pewresearch.org/global/2021/03/18/the-pandemic-stalls-growth-in-the-global-middle-class-pushes-poverty-up-sharply/.

2   The World Bank defines income classes in terms of PPP (international dollars) at 2011 prices. We convert ICE 360 data (2020–21) to PPP at 2011 prices, generate the income groups and their sizes using World Bank definitions and then convert the data for each group back to 2022 prices to determine the absolute income levels of each group. The detailed methodology has been included in the appendix.

3   A small point on methodology—when using data that compares across the years as we have just done in Chart 1, the 20 per cent income slabs (or quintiles) are constructed based on the per capita income of households and equal population in each slab. Analysis referring to the 2021 survey has been done based on total household income and an equal number of households in each slab. There are pros and cons of using each measure and a more complete discussion is presented in the Appendix at the end of the chapter. The differences as a result of using each method are not significant enough to change the outcome of the analysis and the basis for the grouping will be started in each table.

4   Since no data from any survey captures enough of a sample of extremely high-income households (the uppermost tail of the income distribution), it needs to be estimated using statistical models such as Pareto's distribution at the core of the estimation. ICE 360 report 'Rise of India's Middle Class' statistically estimates the upper tail of what it calls the super-rich, defined as the segment having an annual income above Rs 20 million and numbering 10 million households.

5   Metros have a population above 5 million and 9 million in number. These are Mumbai, Delhi, Kolkata, Bengaluru, Chennai, Hyderabad, Surat and Ahmedabad.

6   Tier-1 and Tier-2 towns are prominent hubs or centres of commercial activity. Tier-1 towns are 2.5–5 million in population, fast-growing and on their way to becoming mini metros, while Tier-2 towns are niche cities with a distinct ecosystem of commercial activity. Kozhikode, Coimbatore, Lucknow, Jaipur and Nashik are some examples of tier 1, and Ludhiana, Meerut, Moradabad, Salem, Chandigarh and Solapur are examples of tier 2.

7   Rural grading has been done at the district level. All 640 districts of India have been graded based on twenty-one development and demographic indicators and 160 each have fallen into the first two grades of developed and emerging rural and the bottom 320 into under-developed rural.

8   Ajai Sreevatsan, 'How Much of India Is Actually Urban?', Mint, 16 September 2017, https://www.livemint.com/Politics/4UjtdRPRikhpo 8vAE0V4hK/How-much-of-India-is-actually-urban.html.

9   Micro-enterprises, by definition, have investments of less than Rs 1 crore and a turnover of less than Rs 5 crore. In actual practice, they are much smaller than the ceiling turnover, as the income data for Indian households shows.

10   Any house, where the walls are made up of bamboo, mud, grass, reed, stones, thatch, straw, leaves and unburnt bricks, is known as a kuccha house. A pucca house, also referred to as pakka house, refers to the kind of houses that are designed to be permanent and solid.

11   Formerly chief economist, MasterCard and Mastercard Center for Inclusive Growth.

12   International group that works on 'addressing common conceptual, definitional and practical problems is the area of household distribution statistics'.

Chapter 4: Understanding Consumer India's Behaviour

1   PTI, 'Household debt doubles in FY23, savings more than halves to 5.15% of GDP', *Indian Express*, 21 September 2023, https://

indianexpress.com/article/business/banking-and-finance/household-debt-doubles-fy23-savings-more-than-halves-gdp-8950080/.

2   ‘“How Can World's Largest Democracy . . .”: PM Modi's Pitch For UNSC Membership’, NDTV, 13 July 2023, https://www.ndtv.com/india-news/pm-modi-pitch-for-unsc-membership-how-can-worlds-largest-democracy-4202979.

3   Michiel Baas and Julien Cayla, ‘Recognition in India's new service professions: gym trainers and baristas’, *Consumption Markets & Culture*, volume 23, 2020, issue 3.

Chapter 5: Demand Leads, Supply Lags

1   Some large stand-alone, single-store retailers in big cities are now establishing a few branches and forming ‘mini chains’ usually local or regional.

2   Pooja Sodhi, ‘Transformation of India's retail landscape with the emergence of D2C brands’, *Times of India*, 13 June 2023, https://timesofindia.indiatimes.com/blogs/voices/transformation-of-indias-retail-landscape-with-the-emergence-of-d2c-brands/.

3   Aditi Shrivastava, ‘D2C dilemma: Building the next Mamaearth in a doubly expensive era’, Arcweb.com, 9 June 2023, https://thearcweb.com/article/d2c-mamaearth-in-a-doubly-expensive-era-costs-fireside-kanwaljeet-singh-brands-nXnQ2rgkMv0ku4lQ.

Chapter 6: Passage through India: The Multinational Journey and Lessons Learnt

1   Vimal Choudhary et al., ‘How multinationals can win in India’, McKinsey.com, 1 March 2012, https://www.mckinsey.com/capabilities/strategy-and-corporate-finance/our-insights/how-multinationals-can-win-in-india.

2   Mathew Eyring et al., ‘New Business Models in Emerging Markets’, *Harvard Business Review*, January–February 2011.

3   Nikhil Prasad Ojha et al., ‘The steady rise of MNCs’, LiveMint, 17 May 2016, https://www.livemint.com/Companies/t6wKAx4HAhpl4MKwCY1lJL/The-steady-rise-of-MNCs.html.

4   Sharmishtha Mukherjee, 'Volkswagen's focus on India stronger now amid global turmoil: Thomas Schäfer, global CEO, Passenger Cars', *Economic Times,* 25 March 2023, https://economictimes. indiatimes.com/industry/auto/auto-news/volkswagens-focus-on-india-stronger-now-amid-global-turmoil-thomas-schfer-global-ceo-passenger-cars/articleshow/98982589.cms.

5   Rishikesha T. Krishnan, 'What does it take for MNCs to succeed in India?', *Hindu BusinessLine*, 12 September 2013, https://www. thehindubusinessline.com/news/variety/what-does-it-take-for-mncs-to-succeed-in-india/article23030345.ece.

6   Prasad Sangameshwaran, 'Why Merc Landed In The Ditch In India', *Business Standard*, 6 February 2013, https://www.business-standard. com/article/management/why-merc-landed-in-the-ditch-in-india-104070201126_1.html.

7   Sharmishtha Mukherjee, 'Volkswagen's focus on India stronger now amid global turmoil: Thomas Schäfer, global CEO, Passenger Cars', *Economic Times,* 25 March 2023, economictimes.indiatimes.com/ industry/auto/auto-news/volkswagens-focus-on-india-stronger-now-amid-global-turmoil-thomas-schfer-global-ceo-passenger-cars/ articleshow/98982589.cms.

8   Vinay Kamath, 'Room for growth if consumers take to proper oral care habits', *Hindu BusinessLine*, 8 March 2023, https:// www.thehindubusinessline.com/companies/room-for-growth-if-consumers-take-to-proper-oral-care-habits-says-colgate-md-ceo/ article66592996.ece.

9   Nikhil Gulati And Rumman Ahmed, 'India Has 1.2 Billion People but Not Enough Drink Coke', *Wall Street Journal*, 13 July 2012, https://www.wsj.com/articles/SB100014240527023048703045774900 92413939410; 'Coca-Cola India consolidated profit jumps 57% to Rs 722.4cr in FY23, ad expenses up 52%', ETRetail.com, 2 November 2023, https://retail.economictimes.indiatimes.com/ news/food-entertainment/personal-care-pet-supplies-liquor/coca-cola-india-consolidated-profit-jumps-57-to-rs-722-4cr-in-fy23-ad-expenses-up-52/104903620#:~:text=It%20was%20at%20Rs%20 3%2C192.17%20crore%20a%20year%20before.&text=New%20

Delhi%3A%20Beverages%20major%20Coca,the%20business%20 intelligence%20platform%20Tofler.

10 'Retail plans with Bharti Enterprises "not tenable": Walmart Asia head', *Economic Times*, 7 October 2013, https://economictimes.indiatimes. com/industry/services/retail/retail-plans-with-bharti-enterprises-not- tenable-walmart-asia-head/articleshow/23602321.cms.

11 'Walmart renews bet on India with $16bn Flipkart deal', *Financial Times,* 9 May 2018, https://www.ft.com/content/d78650c6-5361- 11e8-b3ee-41e0209208ec.

12 Soutik Biswas, 'Netflix: Why the world's biggest streaming service is frustrated with India', BBC, 27 January 2022, https://www.bbc. com/news/world-asia-india-60108294.

13 'Tuning into consumer: Indian M&E rebounds with a customer- centric approach', FICCI EY, March 2022, https://www.ey.com/ en_in/media-entertainment/tuning-into-consumer-indian-m-and- e-rebounds-with-a-customer-centric-approach.

14 Varun Mundkur, 'UBER VEHICLE FINANCING: Bringing Entrepreneurship to the Indian Grassroots', 10 November 2014, https://www.uber.com/en-IN/blog/uber-vehicle-financing- bringing-entrepreneurship-to-the-indian-grassroots/.

15 Madhura Karnik, 'Uber in India is fundamentally different from Uber in the West', Quartz, 17 March 2017, https://qz.com/india/926220/ uber-in-india-is-fundamentally-different-from-uber-in-the-west.

16 C.K. Prahalad and Kenneth Lieberthal, 'The End of Corporate Imperialism', *Harvard Business Review*, August 2003, https://hbr. org/2003/08/the-end-of-corporate-imperialism.

17 'External Affairs Minister's remarks at Atlantic Council, Washington D.C.', Ministry of External Affairs, October 2019, https://www. mea.gov.in/Speeches-Statements.htm?dtl/31895.

Chapter 7: Unlocking India's Mass Market Opportunity: Frugal Innovation and New-Economy Digitally Led Models Shows the Way

1 Shankkar Aiyar, 'Domino effect of scale and Indian cost competitiveness', *New Indian Express*, 23 July 2023, https://

www.newindianexpress.com/opinions/columns/shankkar-aiyar/2023/jul/23/domino-effect-of-scale-and-indian-cost-competitiveness-2597565.html.

2   Jonathan Amos, 'Why India's Mars mission is so cheap – and thrilling', BBC, 24 September 2014, https://www.bbc.com/news/science-environment-29341850.

3   Anu Anand, 'Shoestring theory: India's pioneering budget space probe is halfway to Mars', *Guardian*, 2 May 2014, https://www.theguardian.com/world/2014/may/02/india-mars-probe-mangalyaan.

4   Clayton Christensen and Michael Raynor, 'Jobs to be done', *The Innovator's Solution: Creating and Sustaining Successful Growth* (India: Harvard Business Review Press, 2013).

5   Vijay Govindarajan and S. Manikutty, 'What Poor Countries Can Teach Rich Ones About Health Care', *Harvard Business Review*, 27 April 2010, https://hbr.org/2010/04/how-poor-countries-can-help-so.

6   Vijay Govindarajan and V. Srinivasan, 'Could an Indian Hospital Help the US Cut Healthcare Costs?', *Harvard Business Review*, 23 July 2010, https://hbr.org/2010/07/could-an-indian-hospital-help.

7   Avik Das, 'Henry Ford of heart surgery', *Times of India*, 7 January 2016, https://timesofindia.indiatimes.com/business/india-business/henry-ford-of-heart-surgery/articleshow/50475335.cms.

8   Shilpa Elizabeth, 'Chennai tech firm spins a solution for farmers in Vidarbha', *Economic Times*, 10 February 2015, https://economictimes.indiatimes.com/news/economy/agriculture/chennai-tech-firm-spins-a-solution-for-farmers-in-vidarbha/articleshow/46185407.cms.

9   Jency Samuel, 'With Microspin, it is cotton in, fabric out for growers', *Civil Society*, 13 October 2015, https://www.civilsocietyonline.com/business/cotton-in-fabric-out/.

10   To understand the conceptual idea of unlocking growth in a market by breaking compromises that exist, readers are directed to George Stalk et al., 'Breaking Compromises, Breakaway Growth', *Harvard Business Review*, September–October 1996, https://hbr.org/1996/09/breaking-compromises-breakaway-growth.